MINDFULNESS
& PROFESSIONAL
RESPONSIBILITY

Also by Scott Rogers:

Mindful Parenting:
Meditations, Verses & Visualizations for a More Joyful Life

Mindfulness, Balance & The Lawyer's Brain
(Florida CLE Course Book and Compact Disc Recording)

The Mindful Law Student:
Using the Power of Mindful Awareness to Achieve Balance
and Success in Law School

The Six-Minute Solution:
A Mindfulness Primer for Attorneys

Attending:
A Physician's Introduction to Mindfulness
(Compact Disk Recording)

MINDFULNESS & PROFESSIONAL RESPONSIBILITY

A Guidebook for
Integrating Mindfulness into the
Law School Curriculum

Scott L. Rogers
Jan L. Jacobowitz

Mindful Living Press 2012

Mindful Ethics is a trademark of the Institute for Mindfulness Studies and Jurisight,® The Mindful Law Student,® The Mindful Judge® and The Mindful Lawyer® are registered trademarks of the Institute for Mindfulness Studies.

The use of quotations in this book is intended for illustrative purposes only and not to suggest affiliation, connection, or association between this book and the identified source of the quotation.

Cover design and illustrations: Cathy Gibbs Thornton and Natasha Thornton

Library of Congress Control Number: 2012910448

ISBN: 0-9773455-4-0

For information about special law school discounts, send inquiries to contact@imslaw.com.

First Printing, July 2012

10 9 8 7 6 5 4 3 2

For my father, Arvey Rogers, who has shown me
through his words and deeds what it is to live with integrity.
And to the memory of my mother, Susan Rogers,
for revealing to me the insight that allows us to pay attention
to what lies beneath our words and deeds.

———

For my mom, Ruth, whose creative talent and love
inspire me both as a mom and a writer;
my dad, Paul, who is my role model
for living a life of mindful ethics and love;
and my sons, Jeff and Ryan, who make it all worthwhile.

TABLE OF CONTENTS

Foreword – Patricia White ix

Acknowledgments xi

Introduction 1

I. Mindfulness and Legal Education 3

II. Mindfulness: The Practice and Science 15

III. Mindfulness and the Law School Curriculum 25

IV. Integrating Mindfulness and Professional Responsibility 29

V. Mindfulness Demonstrations & Exercises for the Law School Classroom .. 45

VI. Mindful Ethics 97

Resources 103

Appendix A: Class Vignettes 111

Appendix B: Mindfulness Handouts 125

About the Authors 151

About the Illustrators 154

Foreword

Patricia White

*T*his is not an ordinary law book. It does not tell you much about what the law says, nor does it engage in traditional legal analysis. Instead, it sets forth a practical approach to integrating the use of reflective techniques and training in self-awareness into traditional legal pedagogy. It is written for those of us who teach law so that we might enrich the process for our students and for ourselves.

This book incorporates mindfulness into a course on professional responsibility, offering a glimpse into the classroom as experienced by both student and teacher. Scott Rogers and Jan Jacobowitz have thoughtfully crafted the book so that their in-depth exploration of this process may inspire and facilitate a similar integration across other areas of the legal curriculum.

I had the pleasure of observing Scott and Jan teach the Mindful Ethics course that they developed and describe in this guidebook. I witnessed the students engaged in a conversation in which professional responsibility rationale and rules were seamlessly woven together with mindfulness insights and creative exercises that brought the rules to life. The students' feedback and course evaluations indicate that the course material is relevant, meaningful and, for some, transformative. At a time when the need to increase ethical awareness, mindful conduct and civility is a frequent topic of discussion within the legal community, this course makes a compelling contribution.

Scott and Jan have taught their course each semester for the past five semesters; it is among the first to fill, and always has a long waiting list. Having taught professional responsibility many times, I appreciate the challenge of bringing the material to life in ways that resonate with students. In their capable hands, Scott and Jan have developed a method that works!

ACKNOWLEDGMENTS

hen we decided to work together to develop a course integrating mindfulness and professional responsibility, we were excited about the prospect of developing a new curriculum and of integrating our respective expertise–namely ethics and professional responsibility (Jan) and mindfulness (Scott). Our first discussion took place over lunch at the 2009 Florida Bar Convention. We felt an immediate kinship–and deep respect–both for each other and the natural manner by which we traipsed into the other's field. It was this appreciation that led to the belief that something special could come from collaboration.

Wonderful ideas, sincere intention, and deep desire do not alone lead to change–at least not in academia. We pitched the course, the integration of professional responsibility and mindfulness to Patrick Gudridge, Miami Law's Vice-Dean, who appreciated our mission and approved it for the Spring 2010 curriculum. Janet Stearns, our Dean of Students, who had been instrumental in bringing mindfulness to Miami Law, arranged for the course to meet the professional responsibility graduation requirement. Ileana Porras, Miami Law's Assistant Dean of Curriculum, embraced our curriculum and encouraged us to continue to innovate. Our course does not follow the traditional law school model and without the strong and sustained support from Miami Law's administration, the class would neither have come into being nor been included in the curriculum each semester since its introduction. To Patrick, Janet, and Ileana, we are deeply grateful.

In the Fall of 2011, our second semester teaching the course, Patricia White, Miami Law's Dean, attended one of our classes. Not surprisingly, her engaging manner led her to share a fascinating experience she had practicing tax law that dovetailed with the substantive material we were covering as well as the mindfulness insight that has just been introduced to the class. Her interaction with the students is memorable and we are grateful to her for her ongoing support of the class, her comments on an early draft of the manuscript for this book, and taking the time to pen its foreword.

We are deeply grateful to our students for bringing their engaged intellects, creative spirits, and open-heartedness to class each week in ways that allow for enjoyable, spirited and rich conversations and experiences.

There are many others who played a role in our ability to create and develop the new curriculum and share it in this book. We independently offer the following acknowledgments.

Scott: The aspiration of living a mindful life arises out of the observation of those for whom a mindfulness practice has been transformative and who live a mindful life. I am grateful to my teacher, Fred Eppsteiner, whose moment-to-moment presence and the wisdom and compassion of his words, conduct, and smile, has and will continue to inspire me for the rest of my life. That I am privileged to play a role in the field of mindfulness in law is a direct result of those colleagues who have been supportive of my efforts to do so. For making a difference in ways you may not even be aware of, but for which I will never forget and always be grateful, a special thank you to Stephanie West Allen, Fletcher Baldwin, Brett Barfield, Rosemary Barkett, Lee Berg, Bill Blatt, Michael Bossone, Nan Burnett, Ana Maria Candela, Todd Cavalcanto, Doug Chermak, Judi Cohen, Michael Cohen, Robert Coppel, Atara Eig, Arthur England, Fred Fein, Erika Ariel Fox, Gary Freidman, Clark Freshman, Robert Friedman, Alan Gold, Charlie Halpern, Andrea Hartley, Kerry Hunt, Osamudia James, Amishi Jha, Adolfo Jimenez, George Knox, Greg Levy, Paul Lipton, Rhonda Magee, Iris Morera, Chris McAliley, Stacy McCarthy, Gustavo Rabin, Richard Reuben, Len Riskin, Robert Rosen, Arthur Rothenberg, Mel Rubin, Paula Langguth Ryan, Josh Shore, Kat Silverglate, Andy Solis, Barbara Sonneborn, Janet Stearns, Neil Stollman, Lori Tashman, Audra Thomas, Kim Wright, and Bob Zeglovitch.

Jan: I would not be writing about professional responsibility today if Professor Anthony V. Alfieri, the founder and Director of the Center for Ethics and Public Service (CEPS) had not offered me the opportunity to direct the Professional Responsibility and Ethics Program. Professor Alfieri continues to generously share his knowledge and provide me with guidance as well as numerous opportunities to play a role in the professional responsibility community. Cindy Mckenzie, the program manager of CEPS, has been an unwavering supporter and soundboard through out both the development of the course and the writing of the book. My friends, Heidi Murphy and John Crawford, have listened tirelessly to my ideas and frustrations and provided endless encouragement. Finally, to my parents, Ruth and Paul Jacobowitz, who listened, read, counseled and loved me and my sons, Jeff and Ryan Lodish, who have been incredibly patient and proud, I offer my deepest gratitude.

INTRODUCTION

The role of mindfulness in legal education is emerging as an important factor in the professional development of the law student. As legal education undergoes significant changes and law schools grapple with how best to offer students an education that prepares them, in today's rapidly changing world, for their careers as lawyers, mindfulness insights and practices are being looked to for the powerful impact they have across a number of fundamental domains. This is an exciting time to be engaged in this process as we are still in the early stages of its evolution and a growing number of educators are exploring and developing innovative ways of integrating mindfulness practices into the classroom.

As mindfulness is introduced into the law school curriculum, it will find different forms of expression across law school, professor, and subject matter. But if the wisdom of this practice and its long-term viability is to persist, then fundamental elements of a mindfulness practice and the insights that flow from its teaching and practice will need to be preserved. This creates a wonderful opportunity and challenge to those interested in offering a mindfulness practice to their students, and who plan on doing so using modern applications of exercises, and perhaps even modern technologies. There are no ready-made solutions and debate is sure to arise. This treatment offers an application in the context of professional responsibility, drawing upon the mindfulness exercises developed by the Institute for Mindfulness Studies in its work with the legal profession. In light of the significant changes taking place within the practice of law and the ways that rapidly evolving technologies are resulting in new ethical land-mines, there is perhaps no better context than legal ethics in which to explore this timely integration.

This book is broken into six sections, each offering information relating to a piece of the mindfulness-in-legal-education puzzle. Chapter 1 provides a general overview of the development of mindfulness in legal education over the past fifteen years. Chapter 2 offers a basic introduction to mindfulness and a sense of how research on mindfulness both supports its often-espoused benefits and may be helpful to how it is received across various groups. Chapter 3 explores some of the reasons legal educators

1

are becoming increasingly interested in integrating approaches like mindfulness into the law school curriculum. In Chapter 4 we share with you a detailed look at the Mindfulness and Professional Responsibility course we have taught for the last five semesters at Miami Law, focusing on the way mindfulness has been woven into the course materials and learning experience. Chapter 5 provides you with a collection of mindfulness demonstrations and exercises that you can use to develop or deepen your own mindfulness practice and draw from to incorporate mindfulness into your class. Because this material has been adapted from the Jurisight® program and applied in the professional responsibility context, you will develop a sense of how basic mindfulness exercises can be adapted to apply to a variety of classroom settings and subject matters. There are many ways this can be accomplished; the Jurisight method is but one that has been found to have traction within the law school context. In Chapter 6 we share with you an aspect of integrating mindfulness into a class on professional responsibility that we had not fully anticipated; one that offers promise for the inculcation of ethics and a deeply felt sense of professional responsibility among future members of the legal profession.

It is our hope that this general overview of the area, and specific treatment of one particular classroom application, will serve to inform and inspire those of you who are interested in developing or further enriching your work integrating mindfulness into the classroom, help connect colleagues across the country and world who are interested in this area and who each have a unique and important set of experiences and insights to share, and support and nourish the creative and engaged efforts of all of us, as we move forward into this exciting, important, and mysterious realm.

Scott Rogers
Jan Jacobowitz
Coral Gables, Florida
July 2012

CHAPTER 1 :

MINDFULNESS AND LEGAL EDUCATION

*A*t Yale Law School, circa 1998, an extraordinary event was in the making. The seeds of legal realism had been planted in New Haven seventy years earlier, becoming a tour de force in the evolution of law in America. Now another emergent movement was taking root, again at Yale. Although this one had been germinating for at least 2,600 years, it would not blossom in the law until nourished by cutting-edge neuroscience research. Unlike most movements, which have fixed, almost egoic qualities that bind them to specific locales, this one was fluid, its home more akin to the spontaneous landing of tossed apple seeds across the wide swath of the American landscape.

Yale Law School convened one of the nation's first law and meditation retreats in 1998, thereby launching a mindfulness initiative that slowly took root and grew, with varying permutations, throughout the legal profession. At that time, mindfulness operated primarily as a traditional meditative practice, with instruction consisting of the profoundly powerful and seemingly elusive act of sitting, closing one's eyes, and paying attention to the mind's activity. In the intervening fourteen years, a shift has taken place in the way mindfulness is taught, practiced, and ultimately embraced, owing much to the growing body of research on the health benefits of mindfulness programs and the neuroscience that examines how mindfulness practices may change the structure and function of the brain.

This shift entails a softening of the ancient rigors of mindfulness practice accompanied by a growing appreciation and tolerance for the value of informal practices. Moreover, as one, and then two, generations of lawyers and law professors were trained in traditional contemplative practices, and as they incorporated those practices into their personal and professional lives, the natural tendency to want to share them with others surfaced with increasing frequency. Today there are hundreds, if not thousands, of lawyers, law professors, and judges who are sharing contemplative practices with colleagues and students. They are doing so in traditional and contemporary ways, drawing material from a variety of sources, including the teachings that inspired them, the forms they presently practice, and the creative expressions of the practices that are blooming in the garden of their own experience. Some of these "gardeners" love the diversity of seed and growth rates; others are committed to a single strain, patiently awaiting the emergence of each shoot. Perhaps the greatest excitement of the moment rests in how the garden will be cultivated and tended in the years to come.

TENDING TO THE GARDEN

The 1998 Yale Law School retreat was organized by professor Robert Burt with the guidance and support of the Center for Contemplative Mind in Society (C-Mind), an organization that is devoted to advancing the awareness of contemplative practices like mindfulness in educational institutions and across society. Charlie Halpern, C-Mind's co-founder, and author of *Making Waves and Riding the Currents,* is among the most important voices for contemplative practice and the law. Halpern foresaw a program that would invite law students, lawyers, and law professors to sit together, meditate, and explore the relationship between contemplative practices and the law. The Yale retreat was led by Joseph Goldstein, one of America's great mindfulness teachers and a founder of the Insight Meditation Society, located in Barre, Massachusetts.

As word of the Yale retreat spread, a mindfulness program developed by Jon Kabat-Zinn twenty years earlier, called Mindfulness-Based Stress Reduction (MBSR), was making headlines, with a growing body of scientific research attesting to its effectiveness across a variety of health-related areas, including anxiety, depression, and immune functioning. The program, which Kabat-Zinn founded in 1979 as a modern-day means of teaching traditional mindfulness practices, experienced a watershed moment in 1993 when it was featured in Bill Moyers's PBS special, *Healing and the Mind.* This television coverage, which reached tens of millions of viewers and catapulted mindfulness onto the national scene, was made possible, in part, by the efforts of C-Mind in securing the funding that led to the broadcast. At about the same time as the Yale retreat, John Hamilton, managing partner of Wilmer Hale LLP (then Hale & Dorr), accepted an invitation to have Jon Kabat-Zinn and his colleagues at the Center for Mindfulness introduce MBSR to the firm's partners and associates. The program was well received and coincided with the growing interest across many high-stress professions for a set of tools designed to maintain and enhance well-being and performance.

> *We were having a group discussion and one of the second or third year Yale law students spoke about being in this very high-pressure litigious training which called up a lot of stress. And he made the comment that felt like he needed to get angry so that he wouldn't feel the fear. . . . In the course of the discussion we opened up another meditative understanding that actually one can get accepting of the feeling of fear, even though it's unpleasant, that we can open to it and feel it and be with it, and have it not be a hindrance to any appropriate effective action.*
>
> *—Joseph Goldstein*
> **Founder, Insight Meditation Society**

The following year, C-Mind again sponsored the retreat for Yale law students, and invited Hale & Dorr's attorneys and staff to attend. Yale retreats would continue in the coming years bringing in nationally recognized and beloved mindfulness teachers like Sharon Salzberg, and accomplished lawyers with mindfulness practices like Grove Burnett.

During this same time frame, the legal profession was undergoing a shift from one that embraced zealous advocacy through Rambo litigation, into one earnestly inviting back into the conversation the integrity and ideals of Atticus Finch. Perhaps contemplative practices like mindfulness would be one vehicle toward achieving this end.

With this in mind, Steven Keeva, a senior editor with the *ABA Journal*, began interviewing experienced attorneys, defining contemplative practices and how they might inspire lawyers across the country to integrate them into their daily lives for the betterment of one's well-being, the legal profession, and society. In 1999, the ABA published Keeva's now classic *Transforming Practices: Finding Joy and Satisfaction in the Legal Life*. Part II of this important, accessible, and still very relevant book is titled "Voyage of Discovery," and examines seven different kinds of spiritually informed law practices, with eighteen pages devoted to "The Contemplative Practice" and twenty others to "The Mindful Practice."

That same year the ABA published *The Lawyer's Guide to Balancing Life and Work: Taking the Stress Out of Success*, by George Kaufman, a Yale Law School alumnus, whose legal career has included a high-powered and successful practice as a New York and Washington, D.C., attorney. The book offers attorneys a collection of contemplative practices and stress-reduction exercises designed to help them find balance in life. A second edition was published in 2006, including a section titled "The Quality of Mindfulness," in which Kaufman draws attention to *The Miracle of Mindfulness*, a book by Zen Master Thich Nhat Hanh, who has done much to popularize mindfulness in America.

By the turn of the twenty-first century, momentum was building. Law faculty at various law schools had been developing creative and meaningful ways to infuse contemplative practices into their classrooms and law programs. Professor Cheryl Conner, Director of the Clinical Internship Program at Suffolk Law School had begun offering students enrolled in clinical placements an elective called "The Reflective Practitioner." Professor Jacqueline St. Joan, Director of Clinical Programs at the University of Denver College of Law, was introducing students in field placements to contemplative practice to help them integrate their personal and professional lives. And at CUNY Law, where, twenty years earlier, C-Mind's founder, Charlie Halpern, had served as its first dean, Fred Rooney established, in 2001, a contemplative practices program, offering students, along with the CUNY community, the opportunity to learn and experience contemplative practices like meditation and yoga. That same year, C-Mind, which began to hold annual retreats for lawyers, awarded a grant that led to a watershed moment in the evolution of mindfulness and the law. To many it was as if Miracle-Gro had been trucked into the garden. The scholarship was awarded to law professor Leonard Riskin, a mediation and negotiation expert teaching at the University of Missouri-Columbia School of Law (Missouri Law), where, in 2000, he had introduced mindfulness to LLM students enrolled in his "Understanding Conflict" course. Riskin and Daniel Bowling had just begun co-teaching mindfulness and mediation workshops. The first took place in 2001 at the Association for Conflict Resolution's annual conference, and in 2003, they would present at the Association of American Law Schools conference.

Riskin set about to craft a law review article that would introduce legal professionals to mindfulness practices. Students at Harvard Law School felt the article made an important contribution to legal education, and decided not only to publish it, but to make it the centerpiece for a symposium entitled "Mindfulness in Law and Dispute Resolution." The article was published in the Harvard Negotiation Law Review in May 2002, and fulfilled its promise by brilliantly weaving together mindfulness and the law in an academic context that continues to reach legal professionals across the world. That same year, Harvard arranged for Brenda Fingold, an attorney who had been with Hale & Dorr when mindfulness had been introduced there several years earlier, to lead a six-week workshop on stress reduction, meditation and yoga. During this same time frame, Steven Neustadter was offering ten-week mindfulness meditation workshops to students at Stanford Law School.

> *It's developing these skills, the experiences that you have in doing a contemplative practice – the insight. It's getting a chance to sit down, be with your thoughts, and watch them come and go. Just observing. And how you can take that and bring it into your work as a lawyer.*
>
> *—Douglas J. Chermak*
> **Director, Law Program**
> **Institute for Mindfulness Studies**

With the infusion of mindfulness in legal education clearly on the rise, in the spring of 2003, C-Mind organized a contemplative law retreat at one of America's most prominent retreat centers, Spirit Rock Meditation Center in Woodacre, Califorina, just outside San Francisco. The retreat was led by Norman Fischer, the former abbot of the San Francisco Zen Center and an important voice for contemplative practices in America. These retreats would grow and, in 2006, a four-day retreat, titled, "Effective Lawyering: A Retreat for Legal Professionals," hosted more than seventy lawyers, law students, law professors, mediators, and judges, and took place largely in silence. This retreat and many of those that would follow were also led by Mary Mocine, an attorney and Zen priest and James Baraz, a founding teacher of Spirit Rock. Over the years, Richard Boswell, Judi Cohen, Charlie Halpern, Susan Jordan, and Rhonda Magee, among others, would share personal stories on how their mindfulness practices informed their legal lives. While limited conversation (the retreats take place largely in silence) allowed for law-related topics to be explored, even that discussion was cradled in the spirit and tone of the meditative journey. C-Mind continues to conduct meditation retreats for lawyers, law students, law professors, and judges on both the East Coast and the West Coast, and Norman Fischer's work with lawyers continues to this day.

In 2003, Scott Rogers began to speak to students at the University of Miami School of Law (Miami Law) on mindfulness and the law, an annual event that would expand and ripen into the creation of the school's Mindfulness in Law Program in 2011. In 2004, on the other side of the country, Charlie Halpern began leading an informal meditation group at Berkeley Law. And in between the two, at Hamline University Law School in St. Paul, Minnesota, attorney Robert Zeglovitch—a longtime Zen practitioner who has done much work since then to introduce contemplative practices to lawyers and law students—began teaching an eight-week course on mindfulness and meditation to law students.

In 2005, University of Connecticut law professor Deborah Calloway began teaching Contemplative Lawyering, a course that integrates mindfulness practices—in particular, an approach called Vipassana—into the law. C-Mind's popular retreats continued through 2004, 2005, 2006, and 2007, and in 2007, Judge Ronald Greenberg, a regular at the C-Mind retreats, began speaking on contemplative practices at Washburn Law School. Judge Greenberg continues to work with law students at Washburn, offering a growing collection of mindfulness oriented programs and workshops, including discussion on ethical practice and meditation. Meanwhile, C-Mind's popular retreats have continued through 2011.

Shortly after joining the University of Florida College of Law in 2007, Leonard Riskin began teaching "Tools of Awareness for Lawyers," a course integrating mindfulness and other contemplative practices into the curriculum. In the spring of 2008, Scott Rogers held a daylong workshop for law students at the University of Florida College of Law titled "Mindfulness, Balance, and the Law Student's Brain," a program based on the CLE-approved program that first had been presented to lawyers in 2007. In the summer of 2008, Miami Law's dean of students, Janet Stearns, attended a "Mindfulness, Balance and the Lawyer's Brain" workshop and arranged for the program to be offered, as a six-week class, to 1L students as one of the school's wellness initiatives. At about this same time, Miami Law professor William Blatt began teaching a course called Emotional Intelligence as a for-credit class to 2L and 3L students. Jan Jacobowitz, who directs Miami Law's Professional Responsibility and Ethics Program, began conducting Spirituality and the Law panel discussions both at the law school and at legal organizations. At University of California Hastings College of Law, Clark Freshman, who had recently migrated from Miami Law, began teaching "Advanced Dispute Resolution: Conflict, Emotion, Mindfulness, and Lie Detection."

During this same time, University of San Francisco Law School (USF Law) professor Rhonda Magee and her colleagues, Judi Cohen and Timothy Iglesias, began conducting weekly meditation sittings for their students, and Rhonda Magee presented to the USF Law faculty her article, "The Mindful Law Professor and the Challenges of Diversity." That same year, Douglas Chermak, then director of C-Mind's law program who now co-leads the

> *I* wanted to expose my students to the theory and practice of compassion and connectedness, in the hope that I could plants some seeds to grow some trial lawyers out there who would be kinder and more compassionate to themselves, to their clients, to their opponents —to be more self-reflective and to somehow take out some of the conflict and some of the pain found in the trial process that does not need to be there.
>
> —*Professor David M. Zlotnick*
> *Roger Williams School of law*

Institute for Mindfulness Studies' Mindful Law program, spoke on meditation to law students at Golden Gate Law School. Also in 2008, Carol Walsh and Nancy Harazduk began the "Lawyers in Balance" program at Georgetown Law School, which offers students a series of classes designed to enhance their well-being in the midst of their busy law school life. The success of this popular program, which includes a series of mindfulness, yoga, and other contemplative practices, can be attributed to the committed and collaborative efforts of the program's facilitators, who include Professor Jane Aiken, Larry Center, Lauren Dubin, Michael Goldman, Chris Hall, Molly Jackson, Alexei Michalenko, Mitos Parabot, Professor Richard Roe, and Tina Zimmerman. Vanderbilt University Law School, with its "Supportive Practices and Professionalism in Practice" program led by Julie Sandine, supplements its traditional legal education offering with classes designed to foster in its students greater well-being and professionalism. C-Mind's ongoing involvement in fostering growth in this area led in 2008 to professor David Zlotnick being awarded a Contemplative Practice Fellowship to teach a course in trial advocacy that integrates mindfulness concepts and practices to his students at Roger Williams University School of Law.

In 2009, owing to the leadership of Miami Law's dean, Patricia White, Miami Law became one of the first law schools in the country to provide a comprehensive mindfulness practices program to all students, offering a series of Jurisight classes, along with mindfulness seminars, presentations, and workshops. Jurisight,® as set forth more fully in Scott Rogers's *Mindfulness for Law Students,* is a method developed for teaching mindfulness to legal professionals. It incorporates legal language and imagery, using terms such as "Relief from Judgment," "Split in the Circuits," "Hearsay," "Pain and Suffering," "Order in the Cortex," and "Attachment," to creatively impart mindfulness insights and exercises along with neuroscience findings on mindfulness and the brain. That same year, Charlie Halpern began teaching a two-credit class at Berkeley Law entitled "Effective and Sustainable Lawyering: The Meditative Perspective," a course with a perennial waiting list. Berkeley Law students have met regularly over the years to meditate together, and in 2009, a group of Miami Law students, wishing to embed into the law school experience what they learned in the Jurisight class, formed the Insightful Mind Initiative, a student organization that meets weekly at the law school to discuss the challenges of the law school experience and together practice mindfulness.

Similar programs are emerging at law schools nationwide. Examples of faculty who have recently begun to facilitate and support student sitting groups include Mary Delores Guerra, at Phoenix School of Law (Phoenix Law), who began a mindfulness sitting group in fall 2011; Larry Krieger, at Florida State University Law School, who, at the same time, started up a weekly sitting group that shares with students "present moment" awareness practices; Marc Poirier, of Seton Hall University School of Law, who recently expanded an ongoing group to promote student participation; Scott Peppet, of the University of Colorado Law

School, who also began a student sitting group in 2011; and Richard Reuben who, during this same time frame, helped his students form the Mindfulness in Law Society, a weekly sitting group at Missouri Law. Given this rate of growth, student interest, and faculty involvement, it is likely a national student organization will soon emerge.

The growing list of educators who have introduced mindfulness or other contemplative practices into their curriculum is inspiring. Examples include: Victor Goode, who along with Judge Maria Arias, had done much over the years to grow CUNY School of Law's Contemplative Lawyering Program," has begun to offer "Contemplative Practice: An Exploration of Mindfulness and Social Justice Lawyering," which teaches students stress management tools, such as meditation and yoga; since 2008 Deborah Cantrell has been introducing contemplative practices to students in her family law clinic at the University of Colorado Law School; Jason Meek teaches a class on mediation and negotiation at UC Hastings that is infused with mindfulness insights and contemplative practices; Mary Delores Guerra integrates mindfulness exercises into her "Interviewing and Counseling" class at Phoenix Law; and in 2010 Stephanie Phillips and Angela Harris co-taught a course called "Cultivating Peaceful, Ethical Lawyers through Mindfulness Training" at SUNY University at Buffalo Law School.

> *It's hard to be an effective teacher. We bring into the classroom our egos, our need to know everything, our need to be right about everything. We bring in our complex pre-frontal cortex to manage what's going on in the classroom. And all of this is in the mind and so we find ourselves very easily getting locked up in the mind – which is not really where the present moment is to be found. This becomes a barrier between us and our students.*
>
> *—Professor Richard C. Reuben*
> *University of Missouri School of Law*

In October 2010, exactly twelve years after the first Yale retreat, almost 200 law students, lawyers, law professors and judges convened at Berkeley Law, to share their experiences and ideas at a national event, aptly titled, "The Mindful Lawyer Conference." Notably, the plenaries and breakout sessions included science-oriented presentations by neuroscientist, Philippe Goldin, and psychology professor Shauna Shapiro.

11

That same year, Rhonda Magee, Tim Iglesias, and Judi Cohen began teaching "Contemplative Lawyering," at USF, a course that introduces students to contemplative practices and is aimed at helping them cultivate an ethical approach to lawyering. In her recent law review article, "Educating Lawyers to Meditate," Professor Magee discusses her class and offers a comprehensive treatment of mindfulness in legal education and law that readers will find fascinating and informative. Published a decade after Professor Riskin's seminal piece in the *Harvard Negotiation Law Review* and shortly after the 2010 Mindful Lawyer Conference at Berkeley Law, it provides a valuable resource to faculty interested in inspiring their colleagues and administration to integrate contemplative courses into their curriculum. At Florida International University College of Law, George Knox, who weaves mindfulness into his negotiation and mediation classes, introduced the school's faculty to mindfulness in a 2011 faculty workshop titled "Teaching Mindfulness and Awareness Disciplines in Law School, A Cutting-Edge Solution to a Pervasive Problem in the Profession." Also, in 2011, Joel Rubin began teaching "Contemplative Practices and Legal Practices" at Empire College School of Law, and Ruth Vance began integrating mindfulness into her curriculum at Valparaiso University Law School.

In the fall of 2011, Berkeley Law, under the leadership of Charlie Halpern, formed the Berkeley Initiative for Mindfulness in Law, which brings experienced meditation teachers to Berkeley Law and speakers, including lawyers, professors, and judges, who have integrated meditation practice with law practice. In the fall of 2012, students at Miami Law will be enrolling in "Mindfulness in Law," a new course taught by Scott Rogers, which will expose students to a variety of mindfulness practices and integrate mindfulness across a range of legal practice areas.

We conclude this review with a class called "Mindful Ethics: Professional Responsibility for Lawyers in the Digital Age," which we began teaching at Miami Law in the spring of 2010 and is now a mainstay of the school's course offerings. Our curriculum and our experience developing and teaching this class over the past three years forms the basis of this book's specific integration of mindfulness and professional responsibility.

In the twelve years between the 1998 retreat at Yale and the 2010

Mindful Lawyer Conference in Berkeley, many attorneys have coordinated and conducted workshops, retreats, presentations, and gatherings, held in law firms, law schools, at bar meetings and conventions, judicial conferences, and in private settings, all designed to introduce attorneys and law students to contemplative practices, or to create a space for them to deepen their practices. The Resources section provides websites that offer a comprehensive account of these lawyer and law student programs, and of the creative, passionate, and deeply committed attorneys, law professors and judges who have contributed to the evolution of mindfulness in law.

> *We are not here to become great meditators. We are here to become happy people, calm people, peaceful people, centered people, grounded people. These practices are about allowing us to realize the true potential of what it means to be a human being— to be able to manifest the capacity for happiness and well being in our life that is not conditioned on circumstances.*
>
> —*Fred Eppsteiner*
> *Founder, Florida Community of Mindfulness*

As the above survey suggests, mindfulness in law school is reaching a tipping point. Because today's law students become tomorrow's lawyers, it is worth paying attention to what Edward W. McIntyre, president of the Massachusetts Bar Association, penned in 2009. In an article appearing in the *Massachusetts Bar Association Lawyers' Journal*, entitled, "Mindfulness in our Profession," McIntyre called on lawyers to learn more about the role that mindfulness practice can play in offering them relief from their hectic and stressed lives. With an eye on professional responsibility, he concluded his piece with these words: "Beyond such guidelines and efforts to regulate our behavior and manner, each of us has to take the matter into our own hands and be more aware of our professional behavior—be more mindful."

CHAPTER 2 :

MINDFULNESS: THE PRACTICE AND SCIENCE

*W*hen we ask students on the first day of class what mindfulness means to them, they commonly include the word "awareness" in their responses. Indeed, mindfulness and awareness overlap in meaning, especially in the colloquial sense, but the key to understanding mindfulness lies in appreciating the difference between these two terms. The common tendency to equate the two is disrupted when we ask students how awareness differs from mindful awareness, a term often regarded as interchangeable with mindfulness. Take a moment and ask yourself this same question.

A useful definition, crafted by Jon Kabat-Zinn and drawn upon by Professor Leonard Riskin in his seminal 2002 article, published in the *Harvard Negotiation Law Review,* provides that mindfulness is:

paying attention in a particular way, on purpose,
in the present moment, and nonjudgmentally.

Kabat-Zinn's parsed approach helps us to appreciate, at least intellectually, that this thing called mindfulness is more than merely paying attention. It has an intentional quality, is oriented around what is happening in the here and now, and entails experiencing life without judgment (or, as you'll learn, aware of the judgmental thoughts that arise in the mind). If you're like us, you will find something compelling about this definition.

One of the most rewarding aspects of the class we teach is the shift students make from a general sense that mindfulness has something to do with awareness, to an evolving appreciation that there are different ways to experience awareness. In chapter 5, we discuss how we introduce students to different ways of paying attention with a series of exercises that will allow them to deepen their personal connection to the present

15

moment, and to themselves. As students come to live the moments of their lives with a heightened awareness of their experience as it happens, they report that they relate differently to everyday events. Stressful situations become more tolerable, and the students find they are able to maintain the "larger perspective" a little longer than they might have done in the past. They don't take other people's actions as personally. Moreover, students appear to relate more directly to the subject matter of professional responsibility in that

> *M*indfulness meditation is a very simple but not easy way of paying attention. It means to pay attention deliberately, in the moment, and without judgment to whatever passes through any of the senses.
>
> —*Professor Leonard L. Riskin*
> *University of Florida Levin College of Law*

the material is more readily integrated into their knowledge base, and surfaces more spontaneously when they are confronted with ethical and professional challenges.

This book is intended to serve primarily as a guide for teachers interested in integrating mindfulness into their classrooms. Much has been written about mindfulness, and many excellent references are noted in the resource section of this book. For our purposes, the remainder of this chapter will provide you with an overview of mindfulness, elaborating on how it can be applied in everyday life to facilitate a basis for using it in an educational setting.

Mindfulness is a contemplative practice rooted in the cultivation of awareness. A key component to mindfulness inquiry is the mind, often regarded as an expression of the brain's activity. The practice of mindfulness entails learning to pay attention to three primary experiences shared by practically all human beings: thoughts, feelings, and body sensations.

The term *mindful awareness* refers to the intentional act of paying attention, whether it is to thoughts, feelings, or body sensations. By intentional, we mean the quality of awareness that arises when you deliberately place your attention on an object, aware that you are doing so. For example, at this moment you are breathing. In all likelihood, you were not conscious of your breathing a few seconds ago. Now you are—at least a little more than you were before. This marks a shift in awareness. When you bring awareness to your breathing, the activity of your brain changes. Put more squarely within the framework of modern contemplative practices and neuroscience, you are changing the activity of your brain. Brain-scanning technologies that record neural activity as well as oxygen consumption detect this shift. But even more, this change is discernible as a qualitative shift in how the moment is experienced. To experience this more directly, pay attention to your breathing. Inhale with awareness of your in-breath, sensing the rising of your belly or the air entering your nostrils or mouth. Exhale with awareness of your out-breath, sensing the falling of your belly, or the air leaving your mouth or nostrils. After doing this a few times, close your eyes and take five breaths with awareness that you are breathing.

While this instruction is simple enough, there are a great many levels of awareness that can accompany this intentional act. For example, you may have immersed yourself in the experience or followed the instruction with a distracted mind. Perhaps you declined the invitation, choosing instead to read what followed, or doing so with a mind that decided it already knows what it is to breathe with awareness. Above all, did you detect the difference between breathing and paying attention to breathing? By now, your awareness likely has shifted away from your breathing. And now, aware of this shift, you can again intentionally direct your attention back to your breathing. As you have begun to observe, mindful awareness is fleeting.

While awareness of the breath is perhaps the most ancient awareness practice, we can bring awareness—coming to better understand our own mind in the process—with any object to which we choose to attend. For example, look at the book in your hand with awareness that you are looking at a book. Feel its weight as you attend to the tactile sensation of touch where the book meets your hand. Can you sense the difference between the awareness of the book that your brain has noted all along and the heightened awareness you bring to it now?

As we become more adept at paying attention to what is arising within us (the breath) and around us (the book), moment by moment, a world of opportunity arises. The reactive chatter in the mind and the agitation within the body changes. This shift is another element of mindful awareness that we discuss frequently in our course—namely, what happens when we learn to pay attention to our thoughts, feelings, and body sensations. The short answer is that something changes. The more complete answer contemplates the way that it changes, and how this change expands our capacity to act and respond in a genuine way to what's called for in the moment.

Anyone who has begun to explore mindfulness knows firsthand that it takes effort to make that conscious shift, and it is challenging to sustain it. The cultivation of mindful awareness involves a deepening capacity to attend to what is taking place in the present moment. While we might assume we are quite competent when it comes to directing and holding our attention on a chosen object—for example, the breath or this book—the reality is that our ability to sustain attention on an object for more than a few seconds is quite limited. If you are not yet convinced of this very human condition, close your eyes, take ten breaths, sustaining your attention on the breath throughout. What do you notice?

> *The miracle is not to walk on water. The miracle is to walk on the green earth, dwelling deeply in the present moment and feeling truly alive.*
>
> *—Thick Nhat Hanh*

DISTRACTION

Many people are surprised to learn how challenging it can be to hold attention on an object for more than a handful of seconds. Given that we have the benefit of a lifetime of experience, it can be illuminating to discover just how little we know our own minds. If you tried counting ten breaths, you probably experienced some mind wandering. This is quite common. Indeed, our minds are prone to wandering, often without our noticing that we stopped paying attention.

And so a paradox emerges in that the "payer of attention" is the one who becomes "lost in distraction." Mindfulness suggests that we can bring a quality of awareness to our experience that runs deeper than the experience itself. For example, we can feel a hunger pang and "automatically" reach for the Oreos. Or we can feel a hunger pang and "mindfully" be aware that we are feeling a hunger pang. One pragmatic distinction between the two pertains to the decision-making that follows the experiencing of hunger. In the context of professional responsibility, the cultivation of awareness and the reflective capacity to pay attention to our inner experiences without reacting to momentary impulses can have a significant effect on one's ability to act in accord with deeply held values and beliefs.

THE FOUNDATION OF MINDFULNESS

Whereas many contemplative practices have spiritual or religious dimensions, mindfulness embraces a secular assessment of the mind's experiencing of events, oriented around the insight and relief that emerges through this practice. The origins of mindfulness practices are generally traced back to the teachings of the Buddha (a term that means "awakened one"). Modern-day treatment of mindfulness—owing a great deal to thirty years of application and research of MBSR, and ongoing scientific research that delves deeper into the neural mechanisms at play—does not incorporate a spiritual component. Mindfulness practices are acquiring a popular appeal, with growing psychological and scientific interest based upon the effectiveness of these practices as tools for enhancing concentration and well-being. That said, many mindfulness practitioners would posit that their practices do factor directly or indirectly into their spiritual lives. It seems that mindfulness practices naturally fulfill the practitioner in ways that are meaningful to them.

In class, we enjoy a robust discussion of the nature of the mind, with in-class and at-home exercises that facilitate a deepening of this experience and insight. We do not delve into the spiritual or religious elements of a mindfulness practice. We do share information with students regarding the current state of scientific inquiry into the brain, especially as it relates to subjects such as attention, decision-making, empathy, and mindfulness meditation. Below is a brief overview of research that has examined the ways that mindfulness practices may change the brain, intended to offer you just a taste of this rapidly evolving area. In all likelihood, each time you pick up this book, a new development will have been reported in the scientific literature.

THE SCIENCE

As noted at the beginning of this chapter, mindfulness in the West is often regarded as nonjudgmental awareness. The juxtaposition of these two terms—*nonjudgmental* and *awareness*—serves as a reminder that mindful awareness involves paying attention in a particular way, and that something about the way we relate to experience changes as we move into a state of mindful awareness. This is an especially important reminder when discussing mindfulness in the context of the law, or when working with law students or lawyers, who are practiced at focusing their attention in a way that encourages analysis, judgment, and critique. Indeed, it is common for most people to pay attention in a way that emphasizes a critical evaluation of experience, an approach that may have once promoted survival, but today is a vestige that overcomplicates the ordinary.

There is a strong tendency for "non-judgmental awareness" to come across as an oxymoron in the context of the law, where "judgments" serve as the the natural ends of our court battles, and the capacity to astutely judge the veracity of witnesses, experts, and to size up jurors, are attributes of many successful attorneys. But this is not the "judgment" of which mindfulness speaks. (See Appendix B, the "Motion for Relief From Judgment" and the "Motion to Recuse.") These skill sets are more akin to an expression of wisdom and are in sharp contrast to the reactive and defensive "judgments" that arise when we resist what is taking place in the moment. Mindful awareness is noticing that these reactive judgments are arising, along with what are often unpleasant feelings and

> *I'm interested in understanding how the brain is able to pay attention. The main way we have been studying how to train attention, in my lab, has been through mindfulness meditation . . . a mental mode of paying attention in the present moment.*
>
> —*Professor Amishi P. Jha*
> *University of Miami*
> *Neuroscientist*

body sensations, and not identifying so strongly with them that they are accepted as true or permanent. It is one thing to think your adversary is "a lying, cheating, horrible person" and quite another to *realize* that you

20

think your adversary is "a lying, cheating, horrible person." Whether or not it is true, in the latter instance, you have the capacity to make a more accurate assessment and respond accordingly.

To highlight the nonjudgmental nature of mindful awareness is to recognize the various ways one can attend to events arising in the moment. The brain can process information in different ways, drawing on different neural pathways and regions. This important distinction relates to whether stimulus is being processed in an evaluative manner, consciously attending to content, or in a way that primarily engages sensory experience, such that there is little conscious attention to content. Because we can consciously direct our awareness in different ways, we are able to deliberately influence which pathways and regions are activated, thereby having a say not only in the object of our attention, but also in the quality of our experience.

When the Center for Contemplative Mind in Society held its first retreat for law students at Yale Law School in 1998, the discussions that ensued about contemplative practices such as meditation surely addressed the changes to one's mind and body that accompany a meditative practice. These insights were shared largely from a place of personal experience. And, indeed, that personal exploration has been a robust one for thousands of years. Fast-forward nine years to the Institute for Mindfulness Studies' CLE workshop for lawyers, entitled "Mindfulness, Balance, and the Lawyer's Brain," which took place at the Mandarin Hotel in Miami, Florida, in December of 2007. This program specifically incorporated contemporary findings in neuroscience that relate to the effect of mindfulness on changes to the structure and function of the brain. Attorneys in that two-day program learned about mirror neurons, empathy and decision-making, the ways that meditation has been associated with desirable leftward shifts in neuronal activity, as well as the thickening of the prefrontal cortex and insula, the rise and fall of the stress hormone cortisol and its effect on the brain's memory center, the hippocampus, and of neuroplasticity, synaptogenesis, and neurogenesis—the brain's forever-changing nature. The conversation related directly to how one could influence one's neural circuitry and how one's neural circuitry influenced one's enjoyment of and effectiveness in practicing law, and to one's well-being in both life and the law. Today, the integration of neuroscience is found, in one form or another, in a great many programs, both within the law and across related disciplines, such as education, leadership, business, and negotiation.

The last five years have seen the publication of a handful of very readable books that offer a general overview of research into the brain's plasticity, detailing at length the studies that have focused on the role of mindfulness meditation on the neuroplastic qualities of the brain. This research has proven to be a catalyst for an entire movement within neuroscience— namely, "contemplative neuroscience"—and has assumed a major focus in the area of cognitive neuroscience.

> *By bringing science together with meditation, we're beginning to find new ways, in language people can understand, to show the benefits of training oneself to become intimate with the workings of one's own mind in a way that generates greater insight and clarity.*
>
> **—Jon Kabat-Zinn**
> **Creator of Mindfulness-Based Stress Reduction Program**

For example, in 2005, Harvard neuroscientist Sara Lazar found that everyday people who practiced mindfulness meditation on a regular basis had thicker regions of their prefrontal cortex and insula, areas of the brain associated with higher-order executive functioning and the transmission of information between brain and body, respectively. She also found that meditation practice was associated with an attenuated thinning of the cortex with age. Subsequent research by Lazar and her colleagues has similarly reported a thickening of brain regions following eight-week mindfulness trainings.

In 2009, Amishi Jha, while at the University of Pennsylvania, demonstrated that mindfulness practices were associated with changes to working memory and the ability to fend off distraction. Jha has received grants from the Department of Defense to study the effect of mindfulness training on the attentional and emotional capacity of the military, pre- and post-combat, and she and Scott Rogers are beginning to conduct research looking into the effects of mindfulness training on other high stress groups, such as law students. Richard Davidson, who has famously scanned the brains of long-term meditating monks, has found never-before-recorded jumps in brain activity associated with happiness and contentment, as well as attentional skills and emotional stability. His research, and that of others, has demonstrated the efficacy of even short-term mindfulness practices on not only brain states but also immune functioning. Eileen Luders and her colleagues at UCLA's Laboratory of Neuro Imaging, has published a series of fascinating studies on brain changes associated with meditation. These include in 2010 and 2011, findings of increased grey matter, stronger connections between brain regions, and less age-related brain thinning. In 2012, her lab reported finding mindfulness meditation associated with larger amounts of gyrification, folding of the cortex which may allow the brain to process information faster.

To the skeptical lawyer and law student—or perhaps better put, one who prefers that which is familiar and predictable—this science-oriented approach to discussing contemplative practices offers a logical and scientifically grounded basis to justify the allocation of time and resources to its exploration. As a growing number of books, articles, and television specials reveal, mindfulness and attention-oriented practices can enhance one's cognitive functioning and lead to an interest in mindfulness practices as a vehicle for acquiring a competitive advantage in an extremely competitive profession.

We believe that this rapid growth in the emergence of contemplative practices across the legal profession can be attributed not only to the material and tangible benefits they offer, but also because these practices create an opportunity to relax our judgmental, egoically driven way of interacting with others, and treating ourselves. For it is this quality of mindfulness that creates the opportunity to relate differently to challenging experiences, including the conduct of opposing counsel, difficult assignments, uncertain outcomes, and other stressful moments that are inherent in the practice of law. And because a great many ethical and professional lapses can be traced to these events, mindfulness offers a meaningful and transformative way to respond differently, and in so doing, change the course and direction of the moments that follow.

CHAPTER 3 :

MINDFULNESS AND THE
LAW SCHOOL CURRICULUM

Law school education enjoys a long history of training lawyers through the casebook method. Students read appellate cases in a particular area of law, and the principles enunciated within create a string of logical reasoning out of which the law evolves and is established as precedent. Professors "tease" the threads of these cases from the students in a Socratic dialogue consisting of a series of questions that are intellectually challenging; that may provoke a heightened sense of anxiety, especially for 1L students; and that help to integrate this material into the students' growing knowledge of substantive law, rules, and procedures.

As legal education continues to evolve into the twenty-first century, many of the bedrock elements of the traditional educational process are being revisited even as new ones are being incorporated into the law school experience. Law school will always teach the competitive and analytical aspects of the profession, as these are core competencies for the practice of law. However, as reviewed in chapter 1, legal education is in search of alternative and complementary approaches to teaching law, including the development of expanded clinical programs, innovative courses, and a range of new student services. Without question you can look at your own law school for instances of this

> *The growth of meditation courses over the coming years hold such enormous potential for the individual students who will benefit, the clients that they will serve, [and] for thinking about how we make a life in the law even more rewarding than it has been in generations past and how we make the practice of law even more closely connection to the deepest aspirations and the greatest challenges that face our communities and individuals.*
>
> **—Professor Christopher F. Edley, Jr.**
> **Dean, Berkeley School of Law**

We set aside a time to offer guided meditations to our law students to, in a small way, suggest there is more to your life as a lawyer, more to who you are as a human being than you necessarily will be presented with in your classroom space and to provide an opportunity to engage in discussion. We do this to support them in the work they are going to do as lawyers, which inevitably leads to a discussion of the challenges of being a law student right now – the ways in which their values are coming up against what they are learning in the classroom, and how they might more actively participate in the construction of their identity as lawyer.

—*Professor Rhonda V. Magee*
University of San Francisco Law School

change; you may even be one of its architects.

While this change has been afoot for some time, an especially bright spotlight has been focused on the law school curriculum based upon a concern that the legal profession is suffering from a lack of ethics, professionalism, and competence, and that the root of the problem may partially reside within the law school curriculum and culture. The Carnegie Foundation's 2007 report, "Educating Lawyers: Preparation for the Profession of Law," chastised law schools for failing to produce law students that have adequate legal skill, suggesting that the teaching of analytical skills should be complemented with experiential learning in order to increase the proficiency of young lawyers. This finding echoes the voices of clinical law faculty whose work provides real-world experience and practical advocacy skills. Professionalism concerns are being addressed in innovative course offerings that encourage collaborative—rather than primarily competitive—experience. A growing number of courses are emerging that focus on teaching negotiation and mediation skills along with experiential components, and the suggestion has been made that legal ethics be taught throughout the curriculum—or at a minimum, that ethics should be addressed as part of the first-year curriculum.

Among the important changes taking place within legal education and across the practice of law is the integration of mindfulness. As explored in chapter 1, mindfulness classes, presentations, workshops, and retreats are being offered at a growing number of law schools and to a growing body of interested and experienced lawyers, law professors, and judges. An increasing number of student organizations are devoting themselves to creating a space within the law school proper for students and faculty to meet and sit in contemplative silence, and to discuss the ways that contemplative practices can inform the law school experience, the practice of law, and offer relief amid a stressful life experience. Classes are also being developed that integrate mindfulness into substantive topic areas.

> *Students* need opportunities to learn about, reflect on, and practice the responsibilities of legal professionals.
>
> —*2007 Carnegie Report*

In the chapter that follows, we delve into the nuts and bolts of the integration that we have set in motion, namely mindfulness and professional responsibility. We have sought to refine and expand the experiential learning opportunities afforded to students while focusing on the rules, policies, and practical considerations of the substantive material, and to do so in a way that will make a difference—not only in the way students learn the material that we teach, but also across the many facets of their law school experience and into the practice of law.

CHAPTER 4:

INTEGRATING MINDFULNESS
AND PROFESSIONAL RESPONSIBILITY

The decision to integrate mindfulness practices into a professional responsibility course began as an academic experiment. Our hypothesis was that if students learned and applied awareness-oriented skills as they grappled with the rules of professional conduct, the learning process would be enhanced, the students would more readily internalize the rules of professional conduct, and ultimately, they would be more likely to recall and apply these rules when ethical challenges arose in their lives.

The third part of this hypothesis addresses the primary reason for teaching the class—its real-world implications—and also happens to be the least testable. Still, if the learning process were enhanced and the rules more readily internalized, then it follows that the process would have practical benefits above and beyond those otherwise received as part of the classroom experience. As we'll share with you shortly, the anecdotal feedback that we have received from students lends support to this supposition.

Because the integration of mindfulness into a law school's curriculum is a fairly recent occurrence, and little has been written about this subject, especially in a practical, how-to sense, we believe the time is right to encourage and facilitate a conversation about the different approaches teachers can develop and impart in law school classrooms across the country. And because contemplative practices—and, in particular, their application—can be varied and idiosyncratic, we believe that such a conversation will help to elevate this dialogue into a more cohesive, replicable, and even testable body of teaching tools.

In this chapter we share with you the methods, materials, mindfulness practices, and insights that define and animate our class. We present this material in a manner designed to maximize your ability to adapt it to the context within which you teach. While we will break down the course into discrete segments, we think that it may be most illustrative to first share with you the events that inspired our selection of the course curriculum.

A PERSONAL STORY

While the case method offers a familiar structure from which to impart legal rules and reasoning, its omnipresence across the traditional law school curriculum can leave it feeling flat, especially when the material tends not to rise to the level of Palsgraf, the Peerless case, or involve pornography. Resolved to depart from a casebook approach, we sought to infuse our teaching materials with a pragmatic drama to which students could relate. A drama grabs attention, and a captured attention facilitates learning in a profoundly different way. A colleague with whom we had both become acquainted had endured a series of circumstances early in his career that offered a gripping account of the type of trouble a young lawyer can experience with a few unfortunate missteps. We thought his story might serve as a useful teaching tool, and with his permission, we set out to chronicle it.

Our mutual friend Pedro (and no, Pedro is not one of us) enjoyed law school. He had embraced the intellectual challenge from the outset and enjoyed a successful career at the University of Miami School of Law. He adapted easily to the study of law, and was also a gifted writer. Pedro was polite and helpful, pleasant to be around, and generous with his time and talent.

It was no surprise that even in a tough economy, Pedro received and accepted an offer as an associate in a large, prestigious law firm. The shock came about a year into his practice when he was terminated as a result of his role in a complex commercial litigation case. Inexperienced and hoping to succeed in the big-firm environment, Pedro did nothing to stop the wrongful use of inadvertently disclosed documents, the nondisclosure of discovery, and improper contact with witnesses in the case. Apparently, Pedro's easygoing nature and desire to please contributed to his termination. What Pedro eventually realized was that rather than trusting and following his gut, he had relied upon the direction of an experienced partner and her well-regarded paralegal, who themselves had become single-minded in their pursuit of winning the case. In so doing, Pedro closed his eyes to what was happening and hoped for the best.

Ultimately, the partner was sanctioned by the court, subjected to bar discipline, and resigned from the firm in disgrace. Even though Pedro was a young associate and merely "following orders," he was chastised by the judge, his nascent reputation tainted by the event, and at his annual review he was asked to leave the firm.

We suspect that most of you will experience empathy for Pedro and his plight; his is an unpleasant story, and it is easy to "feel" Pedro's pain. So, you may be relieved to know that Pedro learned a great deal from this experience and presently enjoys a successful career in the law, practicing in exciting and cutting-edge areas that might otherwise have been denied him had he remained in a more-traditional legal environment. Moreover, one of the reasons why Pedro rebounded and is thriving is his mindfulness practice, which took root during his third year of law school. This fact provides the link between his story and our class, and why it is that we chose to draw from his story, and that of his colleague, Mindy (again, not one of us), to develop a series of vignettes to introduce ethical dilemmas, guide class discussion, and teach mindfulness exercises.

You may wonder how we can be so sure that Pedro's mindfulness practice played such a pivotal role in his life. Call it poetic license. You see, Pedro—his full name is Pedro Respono—is our creation, and he and his friend Mindy Fuller are the characters that we developed to appear in the weekly vignettes that serve as our primary teaching tools. The creation of Pedro and Mindy offers students likable characters with whom they can relate and empathize. It also allows us to develop (and continually modify and refine) teaching materials that address the specific topics and areas that we wish to explore in class. The students know that Pedro and Mindy are fictional characters.

A Cutting-Edge Context

We crafted the curriculum within the context of social media, naming our course "Professional Responsibility and Mindfulness: Ethics for Lawyers in the Digital Age." We felt that it would be helpful to the learning process if the material was fresh, relevant, and cutting-edge.

Additionally, professional gaffs and ethical blunders are taking place with increasing frequency in this area, and various bar associations and state courts are just beginning to sort out the technological ethical issues and their impact on professional obligations. As a result, we are able to draw upon and introduce into class an endless supply of new articles, bar opinions, and court decisions that wrangle with these issues. And because the students themselves are new to some of these technologies, they exhibit an intrinsic interest in learning more about them, which enhances personal engagement and class participation. Moreover, among those students who have been using social networking services (like Facebook and Twitter), the information imparted about regulations governing professional conduct that may be inconsistent with their current personal use generates both alarm and intense discussion.

Finally, because they are learning the rules of professional responsibility in a context that is constantly undergoing transition, we find that students are more likely to assume personal responsibility for both learning the material and their own conduct; they realize that simply learning the black-letter rule will not suffice, as the rule may change, and its application to a new technology is uncertain. The issues surrounding social media further lend themselves to an emphasis on the importance of mindful awareness in the midst of challenging situations as technology allows for quicker and often impulsive reactions. And, as we discuss in class, these same distracting technologies can be powerful tools to explore and cultivate mindful awareness.

> *I have learned that awareness is important when interacting with the ever-changing online new media world. Awareness allows me to think before I react and gives me the opportunity to determine whether my actions are in compliance with the rules of ethics.*
>
> —*Clark Cannon*
> *Spring 2011*

CLASS MATERIALS

In keeping with the theme of professional responsibility in the digital age, the class syllabus and all course materials are published on a website to which students are directed on the first day of class. This environment allows for the real-time inclusion and updating of information throughout the term as new articles, opinions, and decisions that have a bearing on the course become available. See Illustration 1.

THE MINDFUL LAW STUDENT®
FINDING BALANCE AND SUCCESS IN LAW SCHOOL

Links to Class Meetings
January 17th
January 24th
January 31st
February 7th
February 14th
February 21st
February 28th
March 6th
March 13th -Spring Break
March 20th
March 27th--Immersion
April 3rd
April 10th
April 17th

Final Project

Mindful Ethics:
Professional Responsibility for
Lawyers in the Digital Age

Law 408A: Class Home Page

This course focuses on the ethical implications of the use of social media, weaving into it a review and discussion of the rule of professional responsibility topics and related legal decisions. As mindful awareness is integral to this inquiry, you will be introduced to mindfulness practices, including the associated neuroscience underpinnings, to cultivate greater insight into the personal and interpersonal dynamics that may influence decision-making and conduct.

On the left hand column, you will find links to class assignments. These links will be active the week before the assignment is due.

The pre-class assignment for our first class can be found by clicking here.

Click here to view the class syllabus.

Disclaimer | Terms of Use | Privacy | Contact

© 2003-2012. Institute for Mindfulness Studies. All Rights Reserved. The Mindful Law Student and Jurisight are registered trademarks of the Institute for Mindfulness Studies.

Illustration 1

The home page links on the left side of the page to a series of dated web pages that contain each weekly assignment and all of the information that students will need to prepare for that week's assignment. An example of one such page can be seen in Illustration 2. Each web page contains the same general content, which includes:

1) the weekly vignette;
2) a listing of each of the ABA model rules applicable to the vignette (and, where distinct, our state's rules);
3) readings;
4) homework assignments; and
5) that week's take-home mindfulness practice.

THE MINDFUL LAW STUDENT®
FINDING BALANCE AND SUCCESS IN LAW SCHOOL

Readings:

—Barkett, "The Ethics of
E-Discovery," pp. 80-97.

---Florida Bar Ethics Opinion
No. 07-02
---ABA Article: Formal
Opinion 08-451
---San Diego County Bar
Opinion 2007-1
---Los Angeles County Bar
Opinion No. 518

--ABA Commission on Ethics
20/20 Recommendation
--ABA Commission on Ethics
20/20 Draft Proposal

Optional Materials:

--Outsourcing Audio

Some Relevant Rules:

ABA Model Rules of
Professional Conduct
1.1, 1.3, 1.4, 1.5, 1.6, 1.7, 1.18
3.3, 5.5, 8.4

Assignments:

--Meeting of the Minds
-- Vignette Analysis Form
PDF | XLSX

Mindfulness Practices:

--Integrate the mindfulness
Stop Sign exercise into your
day at a time that you feel
marks an important
transition, i.e., find your own
"Stop Sign."

Class Four: February 7th
"Outsourcing Everything But Your License"
—⌘—

Having been asked to leave the firm, Pedro considers various options and decides to go solo and hang out his shingle. He has a few clients who appreciate the reduced fees and extra attention. Mindy, a loyal friend through it all, is excited for Pedro and remains in close contact with him.

Pedro continues to share his career thoughts and feelings on his blog and others often join the discussion. The blog continues to be a source of support and encouragement for Pedro in his new venture.

However, support and encouragement do not pay the bills, so Pedro commits himself to increasing his book of business.

Friends begin to look to Pedro for help with small matters and old friendships begin to lead to promising clients. One day while Pedro is having lunch with Derrick, a college roommate and good friend, Derrick mentions that his wife, Samantha, has decided to start her own business. She needs assistance with forming a corporation and will need representation with other legal matters. Pedro excitedly offers to help, noting that he had drafted and filed incorporation documents while servicing some of the firm's smaller clients. He meets with Samantha and she becomes his first corporate client. He incorporates her company and she calls him regularly for basic legal advice.

Although Pedro feels fortunate that his friends and colleagues are sending him business, he is also frustrated because of the missed opportunities for additional business; he has turned away potential clients because he felt that the work was over his head. He begins to take CLE classes to learn new areas of the law hoping that he will not have to turn anyone else away.

One day someone from his former firm, remembering that Pedro worked on a big patent case, refers a client to Pedro because the firm has a conflict. The client has a new matter that is likely to be huge.

Illustration 2

A dedicated website has been set up for you to view examples of these pages and to explore their function. Visit http://mindfulethics.com/the-book.html.

In the next section, we will review the primary teaching components for the course—the vignette, the rules, the readings, the homework assignments, and the mindfulness practices—and explain how to integrate these components, thereby allowing for a richer absorption of the material, developing a deeper understanding of mindfulness practice, and fostering a livelier classroom discussion. A sampling of vignettes from across the semester is included in Appendix A so that you may observe the development of the characters across their careeers.

In the final section of this chapter, we will share how we work with this material in the classroom, and the manner by which we hope to have it take root so that it will blossom in our students' professional lives.

PRIMARY TEACHING COMPONENTS

a. *The Vignette*

The vignette students read each week serves to unify the other components of the class experience. In preparation for each class, students read vignettes, ranging in length from one to five pages. Each vignette is crafted so as to include a specific subset of rules. Across the span of the semester, all rules of professional conduct that we wish to explore are contained in the vignettes which collectively tell the story of Pedro's and Mindy's legal careers. More-important rules are repeated across vignettes so that they may be reinforced throughout the semester.

In addition to creating a storyline that explicitly triggers ethical considerations, the intra- and interpersonal dynamics and exchanges embedded in the story are designed to expose and bring to light a range of issues that arise within our inner worlds that contribute to ethical decision-making. These include factors such as "the wish to succeed," "the fear of rejection," "the desire to please," "exhaustion," "doubt," "not wanting to appear foolish," and "uncertainty." As is discussed below, this element opens the door to a fruitful discussion of mindful awareness and deepening insight into the nature of our minds.

b. *Mindfulness Practices*

Each class contains a discussion of one or more mindfulness insights and the teaching or review of a basic mindfulness exercise. As the semester progresses, the mindfulness exercises, which are thematically integrated and build on one another, are further developed as students become more familiar with the process, more experienced with the practice, and begin to appreciate some of the benefits that flow from them. Examples of these mindfulness insights and exercises are discussed at greater length in the following section. If you are experienced with contemplative practices, then applicable insights and exercises may naturally come to you. In the following chapter you will find a collection of mindfulness insights and exercises that we brought into the class and which you may draw from in developing or complementing your course.

c. *The Rules of Professional Responsibility*
Each class web page provides students with a list of the primary rules addressed in the vignette, and each rule is hyperlinked to the specific ABA model rule. Because we teach in Florida, we also provide links to Florida rules when they differ significantly from the model rules.

d. *The Readings*
1) Professional Responsibility–Oriented Readings
The primary required reading is a text containing the annotated model rules to familiarize students with this resource, and to help them round out their understanding of the rules and the larger context in which they are applied. So as to more fully illuminate the rules and their real-life application, we provide links on each class web page to a selection of state bar advisory opinions, court decisions, and/or news articles, blogs, and websites that address the application of one or more of the rules, often in the context of the social media explored in the vignette. See Illustration 2.

2) Mindfulness-Oriented Readings
The primary required reading to introduce students to mindfulness is *Mindfulness for Law Students*. We ask students to not read ahead so that various discussions and exercises conducted in class can be a fresh experience and thereafter reflected upon. The book also offers students a general overview of mindfulness that they can explore throughout their legal careers. In addition, we assign mindfulness readings and materials ranging from book chapters and articles to blogs, videos, and podcasts, most of which are accessible from a link on the class web page. These materials are intended to help elucidate mindfulness teachings and further expose students to neuroscience findings in the area of mindfulness and ethics.

e. *Homework Assignments*

The class homework requires that students apply the rules of professional responsibility in a traditional format that is infused with mindfulness elements. We find that this approach (as elucidated in the following section) contributes to students coming to class prepared and engaged. They integrate the material in a way that feels personal, and, as a result, students are more committed to the process.

1) Vignette Analysis Form (VAF)

Students are provided with a form to complete after reading the vignette and the professional responsibility–oriented materials (the Vignette Analysis Form, or VAF). This form appears in Illustration 3, and is reproduced at the end of Appendix A.

Vignette Analysis Form

What is the Professional Responsibility "Event"?	What rule(s) may be implicated?	Was there a violation of the rule(s)?	Why or why not?	Do you agree?	What was the "Want"?
		1---2---3---4---5 No　　　Yes		No : Yes	
		1----2----3----4----5		No : Yes	
		1----2----3----4----5		No : Yes	
		1----2----3----4----5		No : Yes	

Illustration 3

The VAF requires that students conduct a traditional examination and application of the rules to a specific set of facts. The form resembles a spreadsheet and asks students to, seriatim, identify the events contained in the vignette out of which an ethical issue arises, along with the rule(s) applicable to each event. The form also invites students to consider whether they believe that the rule is appropriate and serves a meaningful

> *Weekly writing assignments and the vignette analysis form allowed me to learn the rules without really having to study them. It is incredible how that happened.*
>
> **—Susie Cantania**
> **Spring 2011**

purpose in the regulation of lawyers. Students are encouraged to explore how they feel about a rule and the underlying policy considerations. This question hints at the indefinite application of any one rule and shifts the student's relationship to the rule from passive recipient to active decision-maker. It also lays the foundation for the mindfulness discussion of how attorneys can, under stressed conditions, act in ways inconsistent with their own values and beliefs. This exercise sets the stage for the class discussion.

2) Meeting of the Minds (MOM)

Also flowing directly out of the vignette is a journaling assignment that asks students to place themselves in the "shoes" of that week's featured protagonist, Pedro or Mindy, as they reflect upon the events that transpired (Meeting of the Minds, or MOM). In their writings, students are asked to make explicit the thoughts, feelings, and body sensations that arise as they imagine themselves caught in the unfolding drama. The assignment allows students to experiment with the range of inner experiences that accompany the various challenging encounters that occur in professional life. As we are learning from the developing neuroscience literature, this exercise may activate neural pathways

> *The journal worked well for me because by putting myself in the situation, I could experience the ethical missteps and remind myself not to repeat the same mistakes.*
>
> **—Lin Zhou**
> **Spring 2011**

similar to those that would come into play were the vignette a real-life experience. We share this with students, along with our intention that they experience professional challenges in the safety of the class, so that the awareness they bring to the event and the manner by which they endeavor to resolve it can serve as a powerful lesson and perhaps even an inoculating force to aid them when similar situations arise in the future.

THE CLASSROOM EXPERIENCE

Each class integrates professional responsibility and mindfulness in ways that allow the two to be explored independently, so that the core insights and teachings can be transmitted in a focused manner, while allowing for the natural and often spontaneous interplay of the two to emerge. To accomplish this, the following class structure is generally employed:

- We invite general questions.
- We conduct a short mindfulness exercise.
- We apply the rules to the vignette.
- We take a short break.
- We explore the role of mindfulness awareness on the vignette's characters and their conduct.
- We introduce a mindfulness insight/demonstration or practice.
- We close with a short mindfulness exercise.

Because the mindfulness material is new to many students, we believe that a predictable flow facilitates the stability out of which the contemplative material may be understood and absorbed with the greatest efficacy. Of course, we do not adhere to this blueprint rigidly, but it often proves to be helpful and effective.

a. *General Questions*
At the beginning of class, we ask students whether they have any questions. We leave this open-ended, and generally the questions that emerge pertain to some administrative element of the class. It is a good way to have students settle into the class and alleviate any minor anxieties that may create unnecessary distraction.

b. *Opening with a Short Mindfulness Exercise*
After fielding a few questions, we begin with a short mindfulness exercise – which usually entails asking students to lower or close their eyes and pay attention to their breathing. This exercise will occasionally be introduced with reference to the material that we are working with in class. For example, if the vignette explores a very challenging episode for

Pedro, we may start the exercise by saying that "we'll begin with a breathing practice Pedro likely would have found helpful given the week's events." We do not assume that the students recollect the exercise or are comfortable doing so—some are while others are not—so we always provide general guidance

> *My favorite part of the day was the few minutes before class actually began in which we would do various breathing exercises. I was surprised how much it calmed me down and actually allowed me to re-focus on what was happening at that moment.*
>
> —*Austin Young*
> *Spring 2011*

during the exercise. During one of the early classes, we facilitate discussion about students' reactions to these exercises and get a sense of the general receptivity and comfort level to assist us in the pacing of these exercises. In the Formal Practices section of the next chapter you can read examples of mindfulness exercises that are conducted at the beginning of class.

c. *Applying the Rules to the Vignette*

The homework assignments are submitted by students approximately four days prior to class so that we are able to review them. As a result, the vignette may not be fresh in student's minds, so we provide copies of the vignette to a handful of students and ask them to read aloud a designated portion.

At this point in class, the students have been afforded an opportunity to ask questions to clear up any ambiguities from the preceding week; the class has experienced a mindfulness exercise to help tone down distraction and remind students of one of the primary aspects of the class; and the core component of the class—the vignette—has been read and is fresh in students' minds. This format allows the students to follow the process they experienced in doing the assignments. They began a week earlier knowing little or nothing about the material. They reviewed the rules and related readings to prepare the Vignette Analysis Form, and then they personally related to the material by journaling the story from their perspective, paying attention to the thoughts, feelings, and body sensations at play. We find that this mingling of learning and experience results in students who are especially animated for the discussions that follow.

The discussion of the rules takes various forms depending upon the vignette's focus and the students' various reactions. For example, a discussion of the constraints of advertising and solicitation rules often results in a debate as to whether law is a profession or a commercial business enterprise. The discussion also serves as a vehicle for raising the underlying mindfulness elements at play. For example, students realize the anxiety that may naturally arise when attempting to attract clients and how that anxiety and a compelling desire to succeed may lead a lawyer to stray from the solicitation rules when engaging in the spontaneity of an online chat room, especially if that lawyer disagrees with the rule.

> *Approaching the Rules of Professional Responsibility from a mindful perspective allowed me to more fully understand the decision making process that can cause a breach of the rules.*
>
> — *Michael T. Flanagan*
> *Spring 2011*

Other topics lend themselves to global discussions that further elucidate the application of the rules. For example, the question of outsourcing includes many of the fundamental professional responsibility rules: competence, diligence, communication, confidentiality, billing, and conflict of interest. Starting with a general discussion of the expanding global economy and its impact on the legal profession encourages the students to recall and apply the rules in a practical context. As discussed below, it also lowers the mood in the room, which prompts us to invite students to briefly pause, bring awareness to the breath, and check in with their inner experience.

Thus, each week is a somewhat different experience, which keeps the students and us looking forward to what arises in a class. While we plan, we always allow the natural flow to guide us, which means that sometimes our original game plan gives way to an unexpected series of "teachable moments," both for our students and ourselves.

d. *Break*

By this time, approximately half of the class period has passed, so we stop to take a short break. It is our custom to open a box of Fig Newtons cookies to share with the students as they enjoy their five- to ten-minute break. We do this to foster an atmosphere of nurturing and safety, to help curb students' hunger pangs, and to reinforce the classroom experience. It also creates an opportunity early in the semester to have the occasional discussion on mindfulness and food, and on the brain, food, and learning.

e. *Apply Mindfulness to the Rules*

When students return from break, we begin the mindfulness portion of the class. It is important to note at this juncture that mindfulness insights and conversation are peppered throughout the class leading up to this time. For example, as discussed above, during the class discussion of the rules involved in outsourcing, students were asked what they thought of law firms outsourcing legal work to other countries. The question led to a discussion on the pros and cons of outsourcing, and, in light of the precarious economy that leaves students (and many of ours are graduating) uncertain of their job prospects, the collective mood in the room dropped noticeably. While this took place in the midst of a conversation on the application of the rules to the vignette, we used it as an opportunity to better understand the connection among thoughts, reactivity, and awareness.

> *The class personalized the rules to each student, and made us think about what the rule meant, rather than what the rule said. And by knowing what the rule meant, I could remember what the rule said.*
>
> —*Ameya Rele*
> *Spring 2012*

To elaborate briefly, we asked students to explore some of the thoughts they were having at the time. We then asked them to close or lower their eyes and pay attention to their breath, noticing how they were feeling, and to the sensations in their bodies. A few moments later when we discussed this as a group, it was clear that the general mood was a somber one. We asked them to consider the extent to which their thoughts might be contributing to their feelings, and how their feelings might be contributing to their thoughts. We also pointed out that a few moments earlier, all was "well," and that a few moments hence, all would be "well" again. Through this exercise students (and teachers) sensed the transient, fleeting nature of thoughts and feelings.

We then asked them to consider whether they had been "aware" of the thoughts and feelings that were arising amid the discussion, or whether they had reacted to them without awareness. Having together processed this integrative experience, we returned to the discussion of the rules.

When the formal mindfulness portion begins, one of the mindfulness demonstrations or exercises set forth in Chapter 5 is introduced, along with an interactive sharing of its insights and discussion of its relevance to the class material or to professional responsibility and ethical decision making in general. While we have connected these demonstrations and exercises to our curriculum, you will find them readily adaptable to your course materials as well. A collection of the ways that these terms are used to introduce mindfulness concepts and insights and tie them to a discussion of professional responsibility is found in chapter six.

f. *A Take-Home Mindfulness Exercise*

At the close of each class, we share with students a mindfulness or awareness exercise that they are asked to practice during the week. These exercises are thematically related, build on one another, and derive from the Jurisight approach to teaching mindfulness exercises to law students and lawyers. These exercises are discussed more fully in Chapter 5.

After reviewing this exercise and discussing times it might be practiced, we inquire whether anyone has questions. As the semester progresses, students come to appreciate the potential for mindfulness practices to play a meaningful role in their lives and careers. Not surprisingly, deeper and more probing questions are raised. For example, as students begin to understand and develop an awareness of the underlying feelings that are contributing to their reactions, they often struggle with how to convert those impulse reactions to thoughtful responses. Sometimes specific questions can be addressed succinctly, with a short

> *I* thought back on the semester and smiled. I thought about the "pocket full of thyme," the "uncertain-tee," drinking tea, the dimes, spirals, snow globes, and how this all related to ethics, to my future as a lawyer and professional, to my future as a person, as a contributing member of society. I realized how just stopping to think and breathe can solve oh so much.
>
> **—Jeremy Kreines**
> *Fall 2011*

43

reply. Other questions require an acknowledgment of the wisdom of the question, and perhaps a suggestion that we "sit" with the question and explore it the following week. Sometimes the question can be integrated into the closing mindfulness practice.

g. *Closing with a Short Mindfulness Exercise*
In an effort to facilitate a genuine interweaving of mindfulness throughout the class, we end with a short one- to three-minute mindfulness practice—often a basic sitting practice. To begin and end with the same simple exercise can be helpful, as students will come to know it well, find it to be a source of comfort and relief, and be more likely to integrate this practice into their life outside of class.

THE FINAL PROJECT

The class culminates with a final take-home project where the students read a vignette in which they play a role as a recently hired associate in Pedro's and Mindy's newly formed law firm. The vignette raises a host of ethical concerns that involve all of the characters. Through this exercise, students are given the opportunity to integrate and apply what they have learned during the semester to a personally relevant vignette. A close look at the students' final projects shows us that by the end of the semester, they have begun to develop an intuitive feel for both mindfulness and the ethics rules. Rather than merely citing an appropriate rule, they describe their initial thoughts, feelings, and impulses to avoid or ignore the rules. They explain how mindful awareness leads to greater insight into their reactivity. Students begin to more readily sense the interplay that exists between ethical issues and mindful awareness. The final project allows them to relate to this integration firsthand, and to formalize its relevance in their lives.

CHAPTER 5 :

MINDFULNESS DEMONSTRATIONS & EXERCISES FOR THE LAW SCHOOL CLASSROOM

*I*ntroducing mindfulness practices into the classroom offers many benefits. These range from creating a more receptive atmosphere for learning to creating an environment that allows us, as educators, to be more attuned to students and each other in our teaching. It also offers students tools that they can bring into other aspects of their school day and integrate into their lives.

There are a great many mindfulness exercises, and they can be creatively adapted to different learning environments. The exercises that we teach in our class have been developed by the Institute for Mindfulness Studies and are part of the Jurisight program. As such, they are geared toward law students, and some of them are especially applicable in the context of mindfulness and decision-making. You can view and listen to recordings of many of these demonstrations and exercises by visiting www.mindfullawclassroom.com.

> *B*y simply learning to notice the thoughts, feelings, and sensations arising in my mind and body, I can avoid a destructive and emotional reaction to them and consciously decide to make a rational choice based on the rules and my own moral compass.
>
> *—Stephen Bacon*
> *Spring 2011*

The exercises we introduce to our students can be broken down into three types:

1) those that offer mindfulness insights;
2) those that cultivate mindful awareness; and
3) those that are helpful for stress reduction.

Of course, the exercises within each group offer elements of the other two, but so that they may be more readily understood, we introduce them with a primary application in mind. Below is an outline of these exercises, followed by a general description. A fuller discussion follows. So that you may have a better sense of the interrelationships among these practices as teaching tools, a suggested timeline appears at the end of this chapter, offering an approach for timing and coordinating them.

OUTLINE OF MINDFULNESS DEMONSTRATIONS AND EXERCISES

■ **Demonstrations that Offer Mindfulness Insights**
  The Snow Globe 49
  The Spiral 52
  Can You Spare a Dime? 57

■ **Exercises that Help Cultivate Mindful Awareness**
  Auto Awareness Practices
      The Stop Sign 61
      The Pretextual Stop 64
      Stop, Look. and Listen 67

  Formal Practices
      Awareness of Breath 68
      Awareness of Body 71
      Awareness of Thought 74

  Informal Practices
      Mindful Eating 77
      Mindful Drinking 79
      Mindful Walking 81

■ **Exercises Helpful for Stress Reduction**
  4-7-8 Hands 84
  The Four Prayers for Relief 86
  The "Just Is" Holmes 89
  The Motion to Embrace 91

Demonstrations that Offer Mindfulness Insights

The "Snow Globe" demonstration offers students a metaphor for the mind that they may turn to throughout the day in order to shift into a state of greater mindful awareness. The imagery offers students a way to tone down their own agitation and reactivity, as well as the tools to help them see more clearly how others can be caught up in reactivity, and how another's reactivity can affect them. As an exercise that offers students a reminder that "we are all in this together," it can help to enhance empathy and lead to greater compassion—for oneself and others.

"The Spiral" demonstration offers students an interactive and lively discussion in which they come to appreciate a fundamental mindfulness lesson: Just about all of our experiences lead to the arising of thoughts, feelings, and body sensations, which, if not worked with skillfully, can result in overreaction and agitation. This exercise alerts students to an important mindfulness insight, and becomes a vehicle for them to reflect on much of their day-to-day experience, especially when they become caught in reactivity.

The "Can You Spare a Dime?" demonstration offers students a perspective for more directly processing the amount of time involved in a short mindfulness sitting and its "intrusion" into their busy days. It also lends itself to the creative development of mindfulness cues that can thereafter be given to students to help them with their efforts to develop a mindfulness practice.

The first two demonstrations are introduced early in the term, offering students powerful constructs for understanding and reflecting on the course material, their own experiences, and their conduct over the course of the semester. The third demonstration is introduced midway through the semester, after students have become familiar with a sitting practice.

Exercises to Help Cultivate Mindful Awareness

These exercises fall into three categories. The first are out-of-class practices that are part of a series known as "Auto Awareness," a name that captures the essence of mindfulness—i.e., awareness of oneself—and are memorable in that they all can take place while driving in an automobile. These exercises include "The Stop Sign," the "Pretextual Stop," and

"Stop, Look, and Listen." Students practice these exercises outside of class, and we discuss their experience with them in class.

The second category consists of three traditional mindfulness practices that involve paying attention to the breath, the body, and thoughts. These are known as formal practices.

The third category consists of the informal practices of mindful eating, mindful drinking, and mindful walking.

Exercises Helpful for Stress Reduction

Students are taught several exercises with an explicit nod to how they might be helpful to them when they are feeling stressed, or how they can produce a prophylactic effect. Most mindfulness exercises can serve this purpose, though it is important to remind students that mindfulness is not a relaxation practice, but an awareness practice. These exercises include the breathing exercise, "4–7–8 Hands" which along with the "Just Is" Holmes can be helpful for working with anxiety and worry; a practice for cultivating empathy and compassion, called the "Four Prayers for Relief"; and an exercise for finding greater relief amid uncertainty, known as "The Motion to Embrace."

In the pages that follow we provide a brief overview of each demonstration and exercise, along with specific instructions to aid you in practicing and teaching them. We also discuss some of the insights that they might offer you and your students. Before we turn to these exercises, we offer an additional insight that we find fundamen-

> *By slowing down my reaction to all that is around me at any moment, I gain insight, control, and of course, empathy and understanding.*
>
> *—Alejandro Miyar*
> *Fall 2011*

tal to our work. If we wish to teach mindfulness well, it is important that we practice mindfulness. Both of us have a personal contemplative practice, and because we teach the class together, in addition to our individual practices, we try to coordinate sitting together before each class. On those days when time is tight, we practice mindful walking on our way to class.

"THE SNOW GLOBE" DEMONSTRATION

Overview:

The snow globe exercise is one that students find extremely helpful. It offers a compelling metaphor for the distracted mind and the benefits that can flow from a mindfulness practice. It also illuminates the power of the imagination to elevate feelings of distress as well as to tone them down. Most stu-

> *When I find myself aware of my inner snow globe, I smile. First because I remember how apt an analogy it sounded in the first instance, but also because I realize that I only remember my snow globe when it is agitated and opaque.*
>
> —*Dale Clarke*
> *Spring 2011*

dents know what happens inside a snow globe when it is shaken: The snow flies. In this exercise, we have students imagine a snow globe with a snowy scene in which a snow man (i.e., snow person) rests in the center.

INSTRUCTION:

Invite students to pick up an imaginary snow globe. Describe the scene inside, with its snowcapped trees and mountains, snow-covered ground, and a snow person sitting in the center. Students will tend to look confused at first, but if you are serious and hold your imaginary globe confidently in your hand, they will catch on and follow your lead. Have them shake up their globe. Then ask them to stop shaking it and describe what they see. They will often talk about how the snow is swirling around.

Share with students the insight that the swirling snow is akin to the "mind" when it is caught up in afflicted emotions, and in reactivity—not getting what we want, learning news we don't want to hear, and even just being surprised by the unexpected.

You can speak of the tens of thousands of thoughts we have each day, many of which are repetitive, and how the flurries symbolize reactive thinking and mental chatter. Students will readily comment on how challenging it can be to drive in the middle of a snowstorm—how it can create confusion, and even be dangerous. A demonstration of this exercise can be found at http://mindfullawclassroom.com/snowglobe.html.

Instruct your students to carefully place their snow globe down on their desk and observe what happens. Most will comment that the snow begins to settle. Invite your students to look closely at the center of the globe and ask them if they recognize the snow person. Some will realize the answer themselves. The answer is, "It is you."

Insight:

1. Everyone has a snow globe, and they are constantly in motion. It can be very helpful to take the time to check in with our own snow globe. By simply doing so, we bring awareness to our inner experience. Once aware, we have a choice: We can either continue to lose ourselves in reactivity, or practice a mindful exercise (e.g., breath awareness) and slow down the reactivity with our snow globe.

2. No one has to physically make contact with our snow globe for it to get shaken up and for the snow to fly; our imagination and how we relate to our experiences is what agitates the snow globe.

3. It can be helpful to check in and notice other people's snow globes. Theirs, too, are constantly changing, shaken up and settling down. Because we are social creatures and our brains are social organs,

The snow globe perspective is such a dynamic way of thinking. In a heated debate I can visualize the other person's snow globe in that moment and temper my decisions of how to react and act (responses and body language) in a way that avoids the situation becoming increasingly serious and uncontrollable.

—Kristen Lee-Williams
Spring 2011

the activity of snow globes can be contagious. Without awareness, we run a greater risk of someone else's shaken snow globe affecting our own. This can include our clients, colleagues, a judge, or our families and friends.

4. As we learn to notice and calm our own snow globe, we offer to those around us a less-reactive snow globe, thereby providing them with a little relief as well.

5. When we put down the snow globe and look at it, the snow tends to settle. This happens not so much because we put it down, but because we are *paying attention* to it.

In Class Exercises:

You can help your students cultivate awareness in their own minds by asking them to check in with their snow globes. Invite them to close or lower their eyes and sense the (re)activity of their mind and body. As they turn inward, ask them to identify, on a scale of 1 to 5—with 1 being "great calm and clarity" and 5 being "overwhelmed and emotionally flooded"—where they sense they are in that moment.

When students use the snow globe to bring awareness to themselves, they can then practice a mindfulness exercise, like mindfulness of the breath, to help calm down the snow globe. It can be helpful to suggest that each time they exhale, they sense the snow settling a little bit.

> *I* am 'carrying' my snow globe on my right shoulder, and many times, when I get upset, I look at my snow globe. It makes me smile inside -- no matter what. It helps to take a pause, step aside, and not react spontaneously.
>
> —*Svetlana Nemeroff*
> *Spring 2011*

Professional Responsibility Application:

When we find ourselves moving into ethically risky terrain or feel a general sense of urgency, hesitation, or doubt, it can be especially helpful to check in with our snow globes. Many ethical missteps might be avoided if we would notice the intense snow flurries and practice this exercise to help settle the snow.

"THE SPIRAL" DEMONSTRATION

Overview:

Life is a never-ending series of events. Our experiencing of these events takes the form of thoughts, feelings, and sensations in the body, which, when ignored or resisted, often lead to distraction and reactivity. This distraction can take the forms of more thoughts, feelings, and sensations. "The Spiral" offers students a memorable demonstration that draws on their intuitive sense of how events can easily spiral out of control, leading to mistakes, overreactions, and unfulfilling interpersonal exchanges, and the ways that mindfulness practices can help them respond more effectively to challenging events. (see Appendix B, page 132).

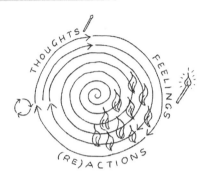

When I saw you draw that spiral on the board it was a mirror for my decision making process. I realized that if I kept making decisions in this manner I was going to be miserable and I would end up making the wrong decisions. This exercise has already helped me avoid making mistakes.

—*Annabelle N.*
Spring 2011

INSTRUCTION:

This effective teaching tool will help students develop a deeper appreciation for the nature of their mind's activity and influence on their bodies, along with the connection between reactivity and the benefits of mindfulness exercises. Students can read about this in chapter four of *Mindfulness for Law Students*. Because of the highly interactive element to this demonstration, teacher training is most effectively accomplished by watching a video or listening to an audio recording, available on The Mindful Law Student website (http://mindfullawclassroom.com/spiral.html). So that the Insights and Application will be more readily understood, please also refer to "The Spiral" illustration found in Appendix B.

1. Invite someone in the class to share a challenging interpersonal experience that they, or someone they know, recently experienced. Write it toward the top left portion of a whiteboard. Alternatively, direct the conversation by giving an example. For example, students well remember the first time they were called on in a law school class. Often, we'll use an example from "real life practice," such as receiving a call at the end of the day from opposing counsel informing you, "just to make sure there's no misunderstanding," that they are not agreeable to the "Unopposed Motion for an Extension of Time" you are about to file.

2. Draw a curved line/arrow radiating out from the "distressing experience" about one-quarter of the way around a circle. Explain that we often have thoughts following a distressing experience, and write "Thoughts" above the curve. Invite students to suggest what kinds of agitated thoughts might arise in this situation. Students will likely respond with things like, "I can't believe she's telling me this now." "She's a liar." "My partner is going to flip out."

3. Draw a curved line/arrow radiating out from the end of the "Thoughts" arrow another one-quarter of the way around the circle, and explain that thoughts can often lead to feelings arising. Write "Feelings" along the curve, and ask them how they might feel in this situation. Students will throw out feelings such as "Angry," "Frustrated," "Overwhelmed," and "Worried." (They will also tend to confuse thoughts such as "Doubtful" and "Wanting to get them in trouble" with feelings; it can be helpful to suggest to students that "doubt" and "wanting to get them in trouble"—while often accompanied by feelings—are perhaps better regarded as "Thoughts." Ask them to tap into the feelings associated with these thoughts.)

4. Draw a curved line/arrow radiating out from the end of the "Feelings" arrow another one-quarter of the way around the circle, and explain that often feelings can lead to the arising of body sensations. Write "Body Sensations" along the curve, and ask them to

describe the sensations they might experience in this situation. Students will throw out sensations such as "flushed cheeks," "sweating," "butterflies in stomach" and "shallow breathing."

5. This is a good point in the demonstration to point out to students that thoughts, feelings, and sensations are continuously arising, and because they are always arising in the present moment, mindfulness practices turn attention to them as opposed to away from them, which might otherwise be our natural tendency. (For clarification, it can be helpful to note that these three responses do not necessarily arise in this particular order, but for purposes of the demonstration, they are listed this way.)

6. Draw a final curved line/arrow radiating out from the end of the "Body Sensations" arrow another one-quarter of the way around the circle so that it almost meets up with the first curve. Explain that often agitated thoughts, feelings, and sensations can lead to reactions. Write "Reactions" along the curve, and then add "(Over)" to the word, noting that these reactions are often "overreactions." Ask them how they might overreact in this situation. Students will suggest reactions like "Yelling," "Saying something hostile," "Firing off an angry motion to the court," "Going home and venting to their boyfriend."

7. Discuss with students how these overreactions tend to be a disservice to their interests and further complicate the challenging situation at hand. Go back to the point between the "Body Sensations" arrow and the beginning of the "(Over)Reactions" arrow and mark that area. Comment on how the mindfulness practices are oriented around paying attention to thoughts, feelings, and sensations because doing so can transform how we relate to the experience, helping us to become less inclined to overreact, or teaching us how to overreact in a less-counterproductive manner.

Insights:

1. The spiral, with all of its drama, sets off an event—nothing more than an event. In this case, it's a phone call with news we didn't expect or want to hear.

2. Life is filled with a never-ending series of events. Most don't register or make their way onto our radar screen—the person ordering coffee as we walk by a café, the pencil positioned on a colleague's desk. But, when the event involves something threatening, generally falling into one of three categories—the unwanted, the undesirable, and the unexpected—we tend to react to it as if it were much more than the natural unfolding of life.

3. In response to events, we experience thoughts, feelings, and sensations. These tend to be pleasant, unpleasant, or neutral. When their unpleasantness rises to a certain level of discomfort, we can react by doing something that serves to soothe the discomfort, offering a short-term benefit that may carry with it a near-term negative consequence. Mindfulness invites us to sit with the unpleasant, rather than impulsively overreact, and notice these experiences. By doing so we cultivate the capacity to bear the discomfort and gain mastery over the moment, with greater choices and more time to reflect. We also learn to fundamentally trust that most thoughts, feelings, and sensations are impermanent and continually in flux.

> *Being* aware of the spiral helps me to keep a positive state of mind by helping me avoid sparking negative situations that will adversely affect both myself and the people around me. I can't tell you how many times since we were taught the spiral in class that I've headed off negativity at the pass, so to speak.
>
> —*Andrew Darby*
> *Fall 2011*

4. Our overreactions, including our words, gestures, and actions, often become someone else's unwanted or undesirable event. This insight emerges when we realize that our thoughts, feelings, and sensations are themselves reactions. You might point to one of the overreactions the students identified, e.g., "yelling," and start a little spiral of thoughts, feelings, and sensations as experienced by the other person. This exercise often results in lightbulbs going off, especially when you link the other person's overreactions to yet another event that continues the original spiral. And so the spiral keeps going around and around until someone gives up, time passes and the situation ends, or . . . someone gets off the spiral so that they can

respond more wisely and compassionately, for which mindfulness practices can be a good start.

5. When you notice you are on such a spiral, a mindfulness practice such as breath awareness can be helpful for moving off of it. Yes, a paradox exists: It is easier to notice that you are caught in a spiral the farther along you are (as distress and suffering become increasingly difficult to bear), while the farther along you are, the more difficult it becomes to move off the spiral. With practice, we can come to realize sooner that we are caught in a spiral, and indeed, by intentionally bringing a mindfulness practice to these challenging situations, our brain's wiring may well respond so as to facilitate our capacity to notice sooner and to maintain our mindfulness practice with greater ease and efficacy.

Professional Responsibility Application:

The adversarial nature of the law, coupled with the unprofessional and sometimes unethical actions of other lawyers, gives rise to events, to which we will want to respond wisely, but due to the "spiral" of reactivity that may ensue, we may instead overreact and become further caught in the spiral. Our snow globes start swirling faster, as do our opponents' globes, and the interaction tends to become less productive and functional than it might otherwise be. Because we are caught in the spiral, and because we cannot see clearly with all the snow flying, we become more likely to experience compromised decision-making, which may involve professional and ethical missteps.

> *Being* able to identify the cycle that leads to this reactive state and also being empowered to stop the cycle is a tool that will be very beneficial for me not only in my practice, but also in my personal life. I believe that if people are able to implement these tools, they will be astounded by the freedom that it affords them.
>
> *—Courtney Daniels*
> *Spring 2011*

"Can You Spare a Dime?" Demonstration

Overview:

The introduction of a mindfulness practice can be challenging, even for those motivated to do so. Sitting quietly and observing the breath can be a daunting practice, notwithstanding the fact that many find it to be a pleasurable experience. Among the various reasons for this is that establishing a mindfulness practice involves replacing something that is familiar and ingrained as a habit with something that seems unfamiliar, and for which there is no established habit.

This exercise is intended to show students how very manageable a short sitting practice is from a practical standpoint. This is important in light of the students' perception that they never have enough time. It is offered midway into the semester so that students can contrast the insight they acquire from the demonstration with the challenges they have been facing in practice. Juxtaposed in this way, students may feel inspired to reestablish their intention to sit on a regular basis, or to deepen their developing practice.

This demonstration will support any amount of time that you have established as an aspiration for your students to sit and practice mindfulness, whether it is one minute, five minutes, or more. The demonstration also creates the opportunity to provide students with simple mindfulness cues you can distribute to them or have them make in class.

INSTRUCTION:

Place on a table in plain view a pile of 1,440 dimes. With at least fifteen minutes remaining in class, ask students to write down on a piece of paper how many dimes they think are in the pile. Collect these papers. On the whiteboard plot the student responses. In our experience, student responses will cluster between 200 and 500.

After plotting and reciting their guesses, inform them that the actual number is 1,440. Then ask students why they think that this quantity of dimes was selected. After soliciting some student responses (which invariably is a source of fun and can be its own mindfulness discussion), explain that the reason there are 1,440 dimes is because that is how many minutes there are in a day.

After this sinks in, pull aside the number of dimes that correspond to the number of minutes you have been suggesting students sit in mindful awareness. Ten breaths can approximate the passage of one minute (or just one dime, to reflect one minute of bringing awareness to the breath). Suggest that the time involved in sitting *takes away* an imperceptible amount of time, and is, practically speaking, quite doable. This exercise is also known as "Breather, can you spare a dime?" Using pennies instead of dimes, you can refer to the demonstration as "A penny for your thoughts."

Of course, this insight rarely dissolves the barriers to a sitting practice. At the same time, it makes the presence of these barriers more explicit, and offers students the opportunity to discuss the factors that can get in the way of their intention to sit becoming a reality.

Insights:

1. Just as we tend to underestimate the number of coins on the table, we tend to underestimate the amount of time we have to get things done, or we overstate the urgency of getting a lot accomplished in the time we have. Just as we have many more dimes than we think, we also have more time than we think.

2. Even with the awareness that we are caught in a spiral or that our snow globes are swirling, the energy of reactivity can leave us feeling that we do not have enough time to practice a mindfulness exercise, like taking a few breaths with awareness. But just as taking a few dimes from the stack leaves plenty of dimes remaining, so too does taking a few breaths leave us with plenty of time to accomplish a multitude of tasks.

Professional Responsibility Application:

When we get caught in feelings of not having enough time, we can feel frustrated and overwhelmed, resulting in poorly thought-out decisions and rash behavior. The knowledge that a certain course of action is the professional and ethical thing to do can sometimes be overridden by the impulse to act quickly, driven by a sense of urgency and the belief that something bad will happen if we do not act immediately. These rash acts can leave us feeling regret for our words and conduct. Taking the time to become more mindfully aware of what is transpiring through a mindfulness practice, appreciating that there is time to do so, can make all the difference as we deliberately engage in a more-reflective approach, less inclined to fall back on impulse.

> *The best way I can describe the experience is this: it taught me that finding moments of peace and mindfulness in the craziness of daily life, even if the moments are brief, can really help me calm down, focus, re-energize, and be more aware and appreciative of the moment.*
>
> —*Austin Young*
> *Spring 2011*

Auto Awareness: "The Stop Sign" Exercise

Overview:

This mindfulness exercise is the first in a series of three that students can practice while driving in a car. The exercise builds on the material addressed in  the anonymous survey, "A Time I Didn't Stop" (see Appendix A), which students complete before the first day of class. This exercise offers them a second glimpse into the connection between mindful awareness and ethical decision-making. Because mindfulness involves paying attention to oneself, we use the term *auto awareness* as a reminder of this turning inward, playing off the fact that the exercise is done while driving in an automobile.

In the survey, students reported on a time early in their life when they did something they knew was wrong but they did it anyway. We ask them to consider why they made the decision they did. A similar situation takes place every day when people approach a stop sign. The law in most jurisdictions is to come to a complete stop, but many people roll right through the sign instead. A rule is knowingly violated.

By bringing mindful awareness into this context, especially at the moment one approaches a stop sign, students gain insight into the thoughts, feelings, and sensations arising in a moment when they are usually lost in distraction, and the ways it can affect them when they disregard a rule. Because coming to a complete stop is an uncomfortable experience for many, the conversation that emerges is often stimulating and enjoyable as students grapple with impulses and

> *When* I think of the experience in the class, the first assignment comes to mind. It was where I came to a full and complete stop at a stop sign. How strange! I paused for what was felt like an unusually long time before proceeding through the intersection. When we got that assignment I thought, what the heck will this be about? However, it soon became clear pretty, and I believe that the subsequent classes helped to reinforce the point. Stop, become aware of your surroundings, think, decide what to do, then act.
>
> —*Dale Clarke*
> *Spring 2011*

motivations of which they had previously been largely unaware.

INSTRUCTION:

1. Form the intention to come to a complete stop when, during the next week, you approach a stop sign. By forming this intention, you shine the flashlight of awareness on your inner experiences and will begin to detect things that previously may have gone unnoticed. You may be surprised by the thoughts, feelings, and sensations to which you gain access.

2. The first step, of course, is to pay attention. To help you do so, when you arrive at a complete stop, take a breath with the full awareness of doing so. Then, proceed through the stop sign.

3. Now it may be that you choose not to come to a complete stop, and that's entirely up to you. Regardless of what decision you make about stopping, this exercise creates the opportunity to notice things with greater clarity.

Insights:

1. Some students will completely forget to do the exercise. This offers an opportunity to convey two important aspects to mindfulness: The first is just how fragile our attention is, and the fact that mindfulness practices can be helpful with training our attention, including our working memory. Second, by sharing this information in a matter-of-fact way, you implicitly model the nonjudgmental aspect of mindfulness in general, and mindful communication in particular.

2. It is not uncommon for students to comment that they become anxious when they slow down at a stop sign, and especially if they come to a complete stop. For some there is no apparent reason for the discomfort, while for others it is attributed to distress elicited by the person in the car behind them, onto whom they project

feelings of annoyance in being behind a driver who comes to a complete stop. As a result of this imagined annoyance, they either do not stop completely, or quickly speed up after stopping. This experience offers the insight that by slowing down and paying attention, thoughts, feelings, and sensations arose in their consciousness that they had never before experienced. It can also strike an "aha" chord as they realize that perhaps their tendency to roll through stop signs might, in fact, be motivated by a desire to avoid the uncomfortable feelings they would otherwise experience—something they never would have imagined as being the reason behind their actions.

Professional Responsibility Application:

Attorneys are sometimes sanctioned for actions that they felt compelled to take at the time, which in hindsight they recognize as inappropriate. In some instances, this poor decision-making at the time seemed the only course of action. And indeed, when agitated emotions come into play, just as with the stop sign, improper action may result so as to soothe the rising discomfort. Just as most students are not conscious of the real reason behind why they roll through a stop sign, practicing attorneys likely do not appreciate the real reason for their actions. Without paying attention to thoughts, feelings, and sensations that arise during these challenging moments, it can be natural to overstate the threat (i.e., so what if the person behind you is annoyed that you stop?) and react with conduct that goes overboard. It takes but a few seconds to stop, breathe, and pay attention—a small price to pay for doing the right thing.

AUTO AWARENESS: "THE PRETEXTUAL STOP" EXERCISE

Overview:

This exercise utilizes a distracting technology—the cell phone. Texting is among the cell phone's most popular features and serves as the foundation for this exercise.

In the law, a "pretextual stop" is one where police power is premised on preconceived bias and exercised with little or no attention to the present moment. Decision-making is often grounded in prejudice, confusion, and even fear. In contrast, in this exercise a pretextual stop is the deliberate engagement of mindful awareness.

This exercise can be practiced both while driving in a car and at other times throughout the day. When driving, the instruction is simply to not look at the phone. At other times during the day, the instruction is to stop and take a breath before looking at your phone when a text message arrives. This is known as a *pretextual search*. Often there are a host of thoughts and feelings that arise along with the sound of a text message's arrival. Many students report an irresistible impulse to look at the text message, unable to pause before doing so. With practice, mindful awareness begins to arise spontaneously, with increasing frequency throughout the day.

INSTRUCTION:

This week form the intention to put a little space between the arrival of a text message and looking at the message. Rather than satisfying the impulse to read the message immediately, exercise a little restraint by first pausing and taking a breath with awareness. Notice the thoughts, feelings, and sensations that arise during the gap you intentionally create. If you are in your car when the text message arrives, refrain from looking at your cell phone until after you arrive at your destination. In addition to being an interesting mindfulness practice, it's also safe driving.

Insight:

1. The arrival of a text message is often accompanied by an impulse to read the message right away. By learning to inject a space between the arrival of a text and its review, we come to more directly connect with the impulse. Students often feel an uncontrollable urge to look at the text and respond. It is not unlike a child who wants to open his birthday presents the minute he sees them. As one acquires greater skill in pausing, noticing the thoughts, feelings, and sensations that accompany the impulse, and resting in awareness for a few moments, they develop greater mastery over their decision-making skills.

2. Unlike more-analytical forms of inquiry and insight, mindfulness practices involve, at the outset, nothing more than paying attention. Bearing the discomfort allows for the development of a deeper level of insight and mastery.

3. In the weeks that follow, we invite students to place their cell phones in the trunks of their cars. Students typically report that doing so "lifted a burden." Because the phone wasn't handy when they had an impulse to make a call or send a text, they couldn't satisfy the impulse, and, in time, the impulse subsided.

> *To me, the ultimate benefit of this class, is how it allows you to have more balance and a deeper understanding of yourself and others. In this respect, it almost seamlessly ties into professional responsibility because sometimes in the legal world you'll have those spirals, and all you need is to stop, take a few breaths, reflect on the situation, and then respond.*
>
> *—Devon Spencer*
> *Fall 2011*

Note: Other exercises that utilize the cell phone and the car involve asking students to explore what it's like to not make calls or answer their cell phones while driving. Of course, this is an important safety precaution as well. If you are in a state that does not allow cell-phone usage while driving, you can modify the exercise so that the student forms the intention to take a certain number of breaths before turning to their phones when a text message arrives.

Professional Responsibility Application:

Reaching for the phone while driving to answer a call or read and send a text—knowing that doing so is dangerous—can be an impulsive act in which we ignore or downplay the danger, all to achieve a short-term gain. By paying attention to this tendency, deliberately inserting space between impulse and action, we notice some of the thoughts, feelings, and sensations that mediate this automatic "reaching." This awareness becomes helpful when we practice law and find ourselves acting on impulse, creating the opportunity for greater reflection and insight.

Auto Awareness: Stop Look and Listen

Overview:

It is important to know what to do when we find ourselves on the verge of making a mistake. This exercise draws on Justice Holmes's rule for what to do upon approaching railroad tracks: "Stop, look, and listen." Absent the reminder, we drive onto the tracks at our peril; or, as a result of distraction, we board a train of thoughts, not knowing where it will take us.

INSTRUCTION:

After stopping at a red light, bring awareness to your having come to a STOP and take a breath, aware of taking a breath. LOOK around you and notice the sights, bringing awareness to the play of light, movement, and shadow, and to the sky, trees, animals, and people. Breathe. Then notice the sounds taking place around you and LISTEN, as if with ears that are hearing for the first time. Breathe. Rest in this awareness until the light changes to green.

Professional Responsibility Application:

Professional and ethical missteps often follow from circumstances and situations that trigger afflicted emotions, such as anger and fear, or agitated and confused states of mind, such as the desire to please. Justice Holmes, himself a model of restraint and reflection, offers the "Stop, Look, and Listen" instruction in the specific context of paying attention to avoid being hit by something you don't see coming, but nonetheless have reason to exercise caution before taking action. Many tough decisions are dealt with in haste. When we realize we are about to cross over train tracks, the opportunity presents itself to stop, look, and listen. In doing so, afflicted and agitated states lose some of their hold on us, freeing us to make wiser choices.

FORMAL PRACTICES: AWARENESS ON THE BREATH

Overview:

A fundamental mindfulness practice is breath awareness. It is among the most powerful of practices, as well as
being perhaps the most simple. It is also challenging.
Because the basic instruction is so simple—Pay attention to
breathing—and because it can be remarkably challenging
to do so, students can become disheartened. After all, they
are used to taking on a task and conquering it in short order.
For this reason we ease into a breathing practice. The first several classes may
involve little more than one or two minutes' attention on the breath—perhaps at
the start and/or end of class. In this way, the practice is less likely to be regarded
as too difficult, or to be found uncomfortable or agitating. As the semester progresses we invite longer periods of practicing breath awareness.

If you are not already familiar with the practice of meditating on the breath,
you will find an enormous number of written and recorded guided practices and
instructions, both from the more-recent mindfulness in law treatments, as well
as the rich history of diverse contemplative-practice traditions stretching back
thousands of years.

INSTRUCTION:

1. Bring yourself into a stable seated posture—not too erect,
   not slumped.
2. Close or lower your eyes, whichever is more comfortable.
3. Bring awareness to your breathing, allowing your belly to
   move with the breath.
4. Maintain your attention on the breath.
5. When you notice your mind moving off in distraction,
   gently bring your awareness back to the next breath.
6. Breathe.
7. Over the course of the sitting, periodically remind students
   to "breathe" or "return awareness to the breath."
8. When you are ready, after one or two more breaths, open
   your eyes or lift your gaze.

The importance of developing your own personal practice is perhaps especially relevant when guiding students through this exercise. This is not to say that you need to be an expert, whatever that may mean. On the contrary; we are always students of the breath and of this practice. But the transmission to students of the power of this practice, as well as the smooth communication of it, follows from personal experience. You will find in the resource section a list of websites that offer audio downloads of a breathing practice, as well as CDs that you can listen to in order to develop your own familiarity with the exercise, as well as your own practice. When you share this practice with your students in class, we encourage you to do so using your own voice, and not through one of the recordings you have enjoyed. Sharing information on one or more recordings with students for practice outside of class can also be helpful.

Note: It can be helpful to have students identify for themselves in an early exercise where they most readily sense the breath. For some it is where air flows into and out of their nostrils or mouth. For others, it is in the throat. Many find it to be the belly as it rises and falls with the breath. By having students notice this for themselves early on, the guided instruction to "pay attention to the breath" will allow each student to attend to the breath in a way that most resonates with them.

Disclaimer: Breath awareness practices are not necessarily for everyone, as some may find it to be an uncomfortable experience. For this reason, we believe it is important to share with students that while you are introducing them to mindfulness exercises they may find helpful, it is for them to decide their ultimate value, and whether or not they wish to practice an exercise they find uncomfortable. To alleviate feelings of guilt for not participating, or of being different from the other students, remind them that the heart of a mindfulness practice is awareness, and not necessarily any one specific object of awareness.

FORMAL PRACTICES

Overview:

Formal practices constitute the most fundamental mindfulness practices, and are intended to be practiced regularly, much like a music student practices scales. Doing so can be a rich experience in and of itself (think Bach's *Cello Suites*), and also serves to reinforce and strengthen mindfulness insights and skills. The following three practices, in which attention is directed to the breath, the body, and thoughts, all involve exercising our attention capacity, and, when practiced regularly, can help to enhance our ability to pay attention. Because one of the obstacles we all encounter when training our attention on an object, or resting our attention on no object, is our mind's tendency to wander, when we first introduce students to a formal practice, we share with them an illustration that helps them to visualize the wandering mind, and offers them insight into their own mental activity.

The "Landscape of the Mind" illustration is found in Appendix B. We ask students to look over the illustration and identify some of the places that their minds turn to from time to time. We acknowledge that the illustration depicts places that we all visit as part of the human condition. These include states of mind such as regret, fear, jealousy, and hope. Drawing on the "Attractive Nuisance" doctrine, we point out that like the poison pool that was so inviting (yet toxic), many of these places draw us to them, notwithstanding the fact that when get lost in them, we can quickly lose focus and clarity, and feel distress.

Through this discussion, we make explicit that mindfulness practices can be challenging due to our mind's tendency to wander. At the same time, based on a great deal of personal experience, along with neuroscience research, through the practice of mindfulness we can gain greater mastery over our wandering mind.

FORMAL PRACTICE: AWARENESS ON THE BODY

Overview:

A related practice to breath awareness is the practice of bringing awareness to the body. With all the talk we do in class on bringing awareness to thoughts, feelings, and sensations, it is through practice that the fruits of a mindfulness practice come to life. Moreover, the insight and wisdom that a mindfulness practice offers—and which can be helpful in encouraging inspired ethical conduct, as well as navigating ethical challenges—flows out of direct experience, which this important and ancient practice offers.

This exercise can be helpful as students grapple with the "Meeting of the Minds" assignment. In most cases, body sensations are the least reported, often left out entirely in the early assignments. Notwithstanding that it can be challenging to imagine someone else's experience, a great many law students simply are not accustomed to bringing awareness to the body. By the end of the semester, students are much more adept at identifying and reporting on these sensations, both in their journal entries as well as in self-reported real-world

I began meditation when I was dean at the law school. A friend of mine suggested it was a way to manage the stresses of this position that I was in. I started with a very simple meditation practice -- and with some real skepticism. It didn't seem likely to me that simply sitting for half an hour in the morning, watching my thoughts come and go, and trying to stay centered and balanced was going to be helpful to me in this difficult job I had. But to my pleasure and surprise, it turned out to be a powerful force. Precisely by giving me a place of stillness and centeredness inside myself, to which I could return in the middle of a confrontation-filled day. I could take a few breaths and come back to that place of meditative stillness. I tried it as an experiment and it paid off for me so I just kept doing it.

—*Charles Halpern*
Founding Dean, CUNY School of Law, and Director, Berkeley Law Mindfulness Initiative

experiences. Students report that this awareness was helpful for them as they got caught in a "spiral"; through a mindfulness practice of paying attention to these sensations, they were able to "settle their snow globe."

I have finally learned to take the moment to breathe, take in, analyze, breathe again, and then move forward. This has kept me more level headed then I have ever been. I was always one to jump the gun, go with the first gut reaction, and live with it. Now I am more deliberate. I observe my surroundings, listening to all of my senses and my body's reaction to stimuli.

— Vinod Bajnath
Spring 2011

As with the breathing exercise, you will find a large body of recordings and writings on practices involving bringing attention to the body. In class, we guide students through a shortened form that has them bring awareness first to where their feet are making contact with the ground; next, to where their bodies are making contact with the chair; then, to their bellies rising and falling with the breath, to their hands, and then to their body as a whole. We will explore variations at times (e.g., the heart, shoulders, jaw), and may guide them through a longer "body scan" in order to deepen the experience, but for the sake of time, and to be able to reinforce a basic practice across the semester through repetition, we tend to limit the scope of the practice to those areas mentioned above.

INSTRUCTION:

1. Bring yourself into a stable seated posture—not too erect, not slumped.
2. Close or lower your eyes, whichever is more comfortable.
3. If your legs are crossed and it is comfortable to uncross them, do so.
4. Bring awareness to your feet, and where they make contact with the ground, or with your shoes. Notice the sensations in and around your feet. Breathe.
5. Bring awareness to where your body is making contact with the chair—your bottom meeting the seat of the chair and

perhaps your lower back, where it rests against the back of the chair. Notice the sensations in and around this part of your body. Breathe.

6. Bring awareness to your belly and the way it rises and falls with each breath. Breathe.

7. Bring awareness to the sensations in and around your hands. Breathe.

8. Bring awareness to your entire body—from the tip of your head to the tips of your toes, from elbow to elbow and belly to back. Breathe.

9. Return awareness to the rising and falling of the belly. Breathe.

10. Direct awareness back to the body sitting in the chair, and to the touch points along your back and bottom.

11. Bring awareness back to your feet and where they are making contact with the ground or your shoes.

12. When you are ready, open your eyes or lift your gaze.

FORMAL PRACTICES: AWARENESS ON THOUGHTS

Overview:

Although not always explicit, mindfulness practices beautifully join concentration and expanded awareness. The concentration practice helps to steady an agitated mind, thereby allowing awareness to expand so that compelling stimuli might be noticed without causing undue distraction. It is all too easy for us to become lost in the stories running through our minds. When we do, we can fall into the spiral, which shakes up our snow globes.

This practice is a primary mindfulness meditation that involves paying attention to the breath and then expanding awareness to attend to the activity of the mind, most notably our thoughts. This exercise is also called the "Just Is Story" as a reminder to students that we are noticing the *stories* we tell ourselves, allowing each one to arise and pass away as it "Just Is." The reference to the great Supreme Court justice can be helpful to students in remembering the exercise, its purpose, and encouraging its practice. While similar in many respects to the breathing practice, in this exercise we maintain a subtle awareness on the breath as we attend to the mental activity arising along with the breath. It is an invitation to cultivate the ability to notice the story without getting lost in it.

INSTRUCTION:

1. Bring yourself into a stable seated posture—not too erect, not slumped.
2. Close or lower your eyes, whichever is more comfortable.
3. Bring awareness to your breathing, allowing your belly to move with the breath.
4. Maintain your attention on the breath.
5. When you notice your mind moving off in distraction, gently bring your awareness back to the next breath.
6. Breathe.

7. Allowing breathing to recede into the background, expand awareness so that you notice whatever thoughts arise in your mind.
8. Breathe.
9. Regard thoughts as you would clouds passing across the sky. Notice them arise and pass away.
10. When you find yourself getting lost in distraction or realize that you had a thought, gently direct awareness back to the breath.
11. When you have reestablished a more-stable presence through awareness of the breath, expand awareness once again and notice mental activity.
12. Breathe.
13. Allow awareness of thoughts to recede into the background as you once again bring awareness to your breathing. Follow the in-breath. Follow the out-breath.
14. Breathe.
15. When you are ready, open your eyes or lift your gaze.

INFORMAL PRACTICES: EATING, DRINKING, AND WALKING

Overview:

We set aside one class toward the end of each semester to focus on mindfulness practices. We call this session a *mindfulness immersion,* and use it as a vehicle to introduce students to other practices that they can integrate into their day. Some of these practices have been briefly introduced earlier in the semester and are reinforced, while others are introduced for the first time. These exercises include "mindful eating," "mindful drinking," and "mindful walking." Below we provide an overview of each practice.

Commonly referred to as "informal practices," they are distinct from the more-traditional sitting practices, and ostensibly less rigid in their application. Still, they are quite powerful and profound in their own right, and, because mindfulness is really a quality of awareness that we can bring to any moment, they serve as important exercises for cultivating mindful awareness during everyday moments.

INFORMAL PRACTICE: MINDFUL EATING

Overview:

Mindful eating involves paying attention to the rich sensory experiences associated with eating. Because eating is such a common act, and one which can be mediated by strong physiological and emotional needs, it can be challenging to slow down and savor the experience. As with most mindfulness practices, the instruction is easy — pay attention to the sights, smells, tastes, and sounds,  and notice tactile elements such as the movement of the hands and mouth and the feel of the food. One compelling feature of this practice, as with the other informal practices, is that it does not involve carving out extra time in your day.

In the classroom, we introduce this practice using a now-classic exercise developed by Jon Kabat-Zinn as part of the Mindfulness-Based Stress Reduction program. The "raisin exercise" is one you can read about on the Internet and in several books. Described below, we use it for two reasons. The first is that it is an exercise most students enjoy and find meaningful. The second is that it is an important prerequisite to the "Motion to Embrace" exercise that we introduce toward the end of the semester.

The exercise begins by handing each student a small box of raisins. We refer to the exercise as a "Ray of Zen."

INSTRUCTION:

1. Look at the box in your hand with a soft gaze. Treat it as if you were an alien from another planet who has never seen one before and has no idea what it is.
2. Notice its colors and shape . . . the feel of the box . . . its surface and edges. *(Try to limit telling them what they should notice, e.g., do not say "Notice the maiden," or*

"Notice the color red," so that they may move into the senses themselves.)

3. Slowly open the box, aware of the intention of doing so, aware of sound and of the movement of your hands.
4. Peer into the box. Reach in and pull out one of the objects inside, placing it in the palm of your hand or between your fingers. (Try not to refer to it as a raisin.)
5. Take your time and explore the object with each of your senses.
6. Your eyes take in its colors . . . shape . . . the way light plays off of it.
7. Feel it in the palm of your hand . . . between your fingers . . . noticing texture . . . size . . . weight.
8. Bring it to your nose, closing your eyes and softly taking in its aroma.
9. Roll it around near your ears (the seeds crackle).
10. Breathe as you mindfully explore this object.
11. (Next they will taste and then swallow the raisin. They can put that raisin to the side and select a new one, or skip the next part if they prefer.)
12. Slowly bring the object to your mouth. Notice the mouth's readiness to receive, or its disinterest. Place it on your tongue, sensing what it is like to manipulate it in your mouth, without yet biting down. (Some won't be able to wait.)
13. Form the intention to take a bite, close your eyes, and, if you so choose, do so.
14 Taste it, and, when you are ready, swallow it.
15. With your eyes still closed, bring awareness to your breathing.
16. Notice your thoughts, feelings, and sensations.
17. Open your eyes.

This exercise can take between five and ten minutes. Allow time for a discussion afterward in which students describe their experience.

INFORMAL PRACTICE: MINDFUL DRINKING

Overview:

Twice during the semester we bring into the class a large pot of hot water, cups, and a selection of teas and healthy sweeteners. We are fortunate that one of the world's finest tea companies, Numi Organic Teas, has generously shared with us a large number of teas each year in support of the Mindfulness in Law Program. The first time we do this exercise is about midway through the semester so that students can learn an informal mindfulness practice they can draw upon throughout the rest of the semester. We also practice mindful drinking during our last class together when we enjoy tea and sweets, and share what we have learned and experienced over the course of the semester—a class that always proves to be a touching and meaningful time for all of us.

INSTRUCTION:

1. Ask students to silently get a cup of hot water, select a tea bag, prepare their tea, and return to their seats. *(We also provide bottled water.)* Remind students that this is a mindfulness exercise, one in which they can bring awareness to the movement of their bodies, the sounds of people walking and of the water flowing, of the warmth of the cup, the aroma of the tea, and the thoughts running through their minds.
2. With everyone seated, guide the class through a sensory exploration of:
   • the feel and warmth of the cup;
   • the aroma of the tea as they bring it to their nose;
   • the thoughts arising in their mind;
   • their intention to taste the tea;
   • the tasting of the tea, with its warmth and flavor;

- the feelings arising within them; and
- the sensations in their body.

(You might find it helpful if you allow your own sensory awareness to guide this experiential practice.)

3. Invite students to take a few minutes and mindfully drink their tea. *(You may find it helpful to suggest that students close their eyes at various points in the exercise to deepen the experience—especially when experiencing warmth, aroma, and taste.)*

4. Allow a few minutes to pass in silence.

5. Suggest to students that their sensory experience is changing, never staying the same for too long. Invite them to pay attention to what "Just Is" changing. *(This can serve as a poignant reminder that everything in life "Just Is" changing.)*

6. Go around the room and have students share their experiences.

Informal Practice: Mindful Walking

Overview:

Mindful walking is a practice that goes back thousands of years and offers students a readily accessible method for bringing mindfulness into their day, both as an informal practice they can draw upon while walking to and from class, or in a beautiful (or 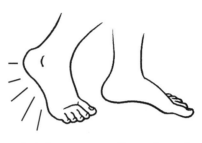 not so beautiful) spot on campus or near their homes, as well as a formal one that can be practiced regularly, much like a mindful sitting practice.

We have shared this exercise with students both inside and outside the classroom. If inside, it is practical to have students form a circle. If outside, students walk in a single-file line to a beautiful area a few minutes' walk from campus, where we then gather in a circle, both to discuss the experience and to guide further practice. Before heading outside, we lead them through a short practice in the classroom. We remind students in advance of class to bring comfortable shoes for walking.

Leaving my car in the parking lot, I walked, one foot in front of the other, acknowledging the traction between the soles of my feet and the hard cement ground. Paying attention to that detail, it seemed as though the walk was longer than ever before. I didn't think about the conversation I had with a friend last night, or what I was going to have for lunch, or how I was going to get through finals. I only paid attention to my walking and the sunshine and greenery that surrounded me.

—Marissa Eliades
Fall 2011

INSTRUCTION:

1. Form the intention to be present for each step you take. Allow your arms to rest comfortably by your side, or with your hands cradled, one within the other. Breathe.

2. Bring awareness to the bottoms of your feet, and to the sensation of the soles of your feet where they touch the ground. Breathe.

3. Shift your weight from side to side, noticing how your body naturally adjusts its balance.

4. Look around you with a soft gaze and notice what you see. Listen to the sound arising in this moment. Breathe.

5. In a moment, we will begin to walk. So that we might pay close attention to our movement and the thoughts and sensations that arise, we'll walk at a slow pace. Be sure to not go so slowly as to lose your balance.

6. It can be helpful to gaze at the feet of the person in front of you, matching their pace.

7. In the event your awareness has moved from the feet, return awareness to your feet and breathe.

8. Slowly lift your right foot off the ground, beginning with your heel and then the toes. Notice how your weight has shifted to your left foot.

9. Sense the movement of your leg as you bring your right foot forward and place it on the ground before you, heel first, then toes.

10. Slowly lift your left foot off the ground, beginning with your heel and then the toes. Sense how your weight naturally shifts to your right foot so that you remain balanced.

11. Bring your right leg forward and place it on the ground, heel first, then toes.

12. With your next few steps, notice four primary movements you are making—shift, lift, move, place.

13. Continue to walk slowly *("in a circle"* or *"like this as you make your way as a group to our designated spot outside")*, mindful of the experience. No rush. Take your time. Allow your breathing to flow with each step you take.

MINDFULNESS EXERCISES HELPFUL FOR STRESS REDUCTION

Overview:

One of the paradoxes of a mindfulness practice is that although it is often looked to for relaxation and stress reduction, it is primarily a practice of alertness and openness to present-moment experience, which has no explicit objective. Yet through this object-less practice, resistance to unwanted and undesirable events soften, out of which a more-relaxed and less-stressful state may emerge. In the language of Jurisight, we see the world as it "Just Is," less inclined to judge it as good or bad, right or wrong, and thereby we become better equipped to move into the next moment with clarity, compassion, and courage.

> *This class was so much more than typical legal education development; it was mental conditioning for a world we face beyond the scope of the courtroom.*
>
> —*Ryan Klarberg*
> *Fall 2011*

While we share this insight with our students, both as a way to regulate expectations and inspire a more deeply felt sense of adventure in the mindfulness journey, we also offer them exercises that explicitly advance a stress-reduction objective. The following four exercises serve this purpose from four different perspectives, allowing students to draw on different ones at different times. The first is a breathing practice, the second is an awareness practice, the third is a compassion practice, and the fourth is an insight practice.

STRESS REDUCTION: "4-7-8 HANDS"

Overview:

This exercise is a basic mindfulness practice that incorporates awareness of breath and body. It is a primary Jurisight exercise and one of the first we teach students. Referred to as a "Learned Hand" exercise, students find that it's easily memorized, and one that can be practiced in a few seconds, both during times of calm and when in the midst of a challenge.

The breathing portion has been found to be effective in the medical community in dealing with anxiety and panic, and we share with students that they may find this exercise helpful for everyday stress reduction.

> *As I sat waiting for the bar exam proctor to tell us to open our test booklets, I felt the stress building. I decided to quietly do the 4-7-8 Hands exercise, shifting my mind to concentrate on my breathing, rather than focusing on my watch counting down the minutes. The exercise allowed me to focus more effectively on the task at hand.*
>
> —*Regan Kruse*
> *Spring 2010*

Students find this a strong incentive to practice, and over the years many have reported that it was quite helpful when they experienced challenging and stressful situations at school, while interviewing for jobs, and, after graduation, when practicing law.

This exercise is best taught by first describing it to your students, then demonstrating it to them, and then guiding them through it. It is helpful if students keep their eyes open while learning it. While we generally practice it while seated, it can be practiced in any position, at almost any time.

Separate instructions are given for the hands and the breath so you can describe and then practice each first before putting them together. As noted below, the movement of both breath and hands follows a 4–7–8 count.

The Breath:

Inhale to the count of four. Hold your breath to the count of seven. Exhale to the count of eight. If comfortable, inhale through the nose and exhale through the mouth, as if blowing through a straw.

The Hands:

Begin with your hands in a loose grip, then fully extending your fingers to the count of four. Hold your fingers stretched open to the count of seven. Close your fingers, returning to a loose grip to the count of eight.

INSTRUCTION:

1. Sit in a chair with your hands resting on your lap, palms face up in a gentle grip.
2. Bring awareness to your hands and to your breathing.
3. Inhale and extend your fingers fully to the count of four.
4. Hold your breath and keep your fingers extended to the count of seven.
5. Exhale and close your hands to the count of eight.
6. Close your eyes or lower your gaze and rest in awareness of breathing.
7. When you are ready, open your eyes or lift your gaze.

We guide students through two repetitions of this exercise and suggest they do the same when they practice it on their own. So that they may more readily commit the exercise to memory, we hand out instruction cards. (You may request a set of cards for your class at no charge, by contacting us.)

STRESS REDUCTION: THE FOUR PRAYERS FOR RELIEF

Overview:

This exercise is regarded as a breath of fresh air for many, especially in the context of the competitive law school environment. It is one that involves the cultivation of compassion, both for oneself and others. We gen-

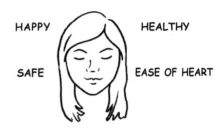

HAPPY   HEALTHY

SAFE   EASE OF HEART

erally introduce it toward the end of the semester after the class has become a close-knit group, but occasionally do so earlier if a class discussion naturally lends itself to demonstration of the exercise. We recommend that you practice this exercise daily for a few weeks before sharing it with your class so that you will have direct knowledge of its impact and may speak to your personal experience, for example, as a tool for 1) fostering a sense of ease in the midst of a challenging interpersonal situation; 2) defusing a grudge or feelings of anger that one is holding toward another; and 3) forging a sense of connection and collaboration.

Because the content of this exercise can be viewed by some as contrary to the spirit of the competitive law school and legal practice environment, we quote passages by notable figures that speak to the importance of connection, or introduce neuroscience findings that may inspire a

One day I experienced one of those devastating moments where you feel like the rug has been pulled out from under you. But the most extraordinary thing happened in that moment. I was expecting my snow globe to start spinning around like a whirlwind and then explode. But instead there was silence. I thought to myself 'well that's rather odd... maybe I just feel too overwhelmed to feel anything' but instead of starting the process which would have led me into the spiral I did the meditation exercise we did in class where you asked us to say "May I be safe, May I be happy, May I be healthy, May I live with ease of heart." And then I repeated it for someone I loved, someone I had seen that day and then for everyone. I opened my eyes and said to myself "that was not your path and you now get to decide to do something different.

—Annabelle N.
Spring 2011

compassion practice. For example, you may wish to introduce a quote from Albert Einstein on how our sense of separateness from one another is an "optical delusion of consciousness," or research from the laboratory of Richard Davidson on how compassion-oriented meditations are associated with interesting changes in brain-wave activity (see Resources). The Four Prayers for Relief are kind wishes we offer to ourselves first, then to three specific persons, and then to all beings.

INSTRUCTION:

1. Find a comfortable seated posture.
2. Lower or close your eyes and bring awareness to your breathing.
3. Bring to mind an image or sense of yourself in this moment.
4. Silently wish for yourself:
   - *May I be happy.*
   - *May I be healthy.*
   - *May I be safe.*
   - *May I live with ease of heart.*
5. Breathe.
6. Bring to mind a person who has been very wonderful to you in your life and cares for you deeply.
7. Wish for this person:
   - *May you be happy.*
   - *May you be healthy.*
   - *May you be safe.*
   - *May you live with ease of heart.*
8. Breathe.
9. Bring to mind someone whom you have no regard for one way or another—perhaps someone you passed by this morning or see on a regular basis but is fairly neutral to you.
10. Wish for this person:
    - *May you be happy.*
    - *May you be healthy.*

- *May you be safe.*
- *May you live with ease of heart.*
11. Breathe.
12. Bring to mind someone with whom you have, or are having, a difficult time.
13. Wish for this person:
    - *May you be happy.*
    - *May you be healthy.*
    - *May you be safe.*
    - *May you live with ease of heart.*
14. Breathe.
15. Bring to mind all living beings.
16. Wish for all beings:
    - *May all beings be happy.*
    - *May all beings be healthy.*
    - *May all beings be safe.*
    - *May all beings live with ease of heart.*
17. Breathe.
18. When you are ready, open your eyes or lift your gaze.

Known more traditionally as a loving-kindness practice, much has been written about its benefits. As students enter the practice of law and experience its stressors, along with the widespread lack of civility, this exercise can prove to be extremely helpful to them as they navigate this challenging interpersonal terrain. Because there is a natural tendency to respond in kind, this practice can help tone down the agitated snow globe that that can lead not only to unprofessional conduct, as an expression of tit for tat, but tremendous dissatisfaction with the practice of law.

Note: Sometimes we modify the last verse by inviting students to bring to mind their classmates.

STRESS REDUCTION: THE JUST IS HOLMES

Overview:

The "Just Is" Holmes exercise can be practiced on a regular basis to help deepen one's mindfulness skills. It can also be practiced during times of challenge, bringing about a sense of relief, especially when one is caught in the grip of anxious thoughts. The exercise is similar to the "Three-Minute Breathing Space" exercise developed as part of the Mindfulness-Based Cognitive Therapy program. A variant of the "Stop, Look, and Listen" practice discussed earlier in this chapter, this exercise shares the same instruction to stop, look, and listen, but differs in that the "look" portion entails looking within, as opposed to looking at what is taking place within one's visual field.

> *I* think mindfulness, and our class, is about accepting the fact that we, as humans, are afraid of change and of unforeseen events. Yet, life is full of surprises. The practice of mindfulness is just this; being aware of this fear of the unexpected; aware of our reactions to this fear and particular situations; and aware of how our reactions affect our lives and the lives of those around us.
>
> *—Sergio M. Eslait*
> *Fall 2011*

The name of the exercise draws on the Jurisight teaching that if we wish to help bring about justice, it is helpful to see the world as it "just is." The alternative is to resist what is taking place in the present moment and overreact or unnecessarily suffer, or both.

INSTRUCTION

Guide your students though this exercise, allowing about a minute for each of the three sections.

1) **Stop:** Close your eyes and bring awareness to your breathing. Bring awareness to your belly, noticing how it rises and falls with each breath. . . . No need to breathe a certain way; simply notice the breathing that Just Is happening in this moment. . . .

2) **Look:** Allow awareness of breathing to move into the background as you pay attention to the thoughts arising in your mind. No need to try to generate thoughts . . . They will arise and pass away, like clouds drifting across the sky. . . . Notice what Just Is arising in this moment . . . . Breathe. If you find yourself getting caught in the content of a thought, compelling as it may be, it is just a thought, just another cloud. . . . Gently bring your attention back to the breath for a few moments, and then once again notice the arising and passing away of thoughts. . . . Breathe.

3) **Listen:** As you breathe, allow awareness of thought to recede into the background and expand your awareness outward, listening to the sounds around you. Pay attention with ears that are open to the mystery of the sound that Just Is—noticing what arises, changes, and passes away . . . sounds nearby and faraway. . . . Open awareness to the symphony of sound.

Gently allow awareness of sound to recede into the background as you once again pay attention to breathing. . . . Rest in awareness of breathing for a few moments and then, when you are ready, open your eyes.

❖

STRESS REDUCTION: MOTION TO EMBRACE (LIFE'S UNCERTAIN-TEES)

Overview:

The "Motion to Embrace" exercise provides a classroom experience that students always find to be enjoyable, offering a few surprises that deepen mindfulness teachings. This exercise helps students to relate to uncertainty with greater confidence and courage.

In the context of professional responsibility and ethical decision-making, students come to appreciate over the course of the semester that ethical missteps may be occasioned by a discomfort that arises alongside uncertainty, and an impulsive effort to reduce that discomfort. This exercise is introduced toward the end of the semester for a variety of reasons. First, the mindful eating (raisin) exercise primes expectations that set in motion a fuller appreciation of the experience and insights that flow from this exercise. In addition, the exercise brings together a series of concepts and practices we have shared with students throughout the semester. Also, the exercise offers students a tangible mindfulness cue that they can take with them and draw upon throughout the remainder of their law school careers, and throughout their legal practice. The exercise is a popular one, and students often ask for extra "cues" to share with a family member or friend.

> *I find it useful that this course has explored the uncertainties of life. It is impossible to predict the outcome of every case or anticipate every challenge that may come your way. This class has made me more comfortable with not knowing the answer to everything.*
>
> —*Liana Nealon*
> *Spring 2012*

In Appendix B you will find a copy of the "Motion to Embrace (Life's Uncertainties)" and the accompanying "Some of Life's Uncertain Tees" illustration. As a purchaser of this book, you are authorized to make copies of these two pages for distribution to the students in your class. You may also contact Scott Rogers to order a full-color card containing the motion and the illustration, along with an "uncertain tee."

INSTRUCTION

If you have previously shared with students the raisin exercise and have obtained the physical "Uncertain Tees," then you will want to prep for this exercise by placing a tee in an empty raisin box. The tees will snugly fit into the small boxes, giving the impression that they are empty. If you are not using the actual tees, then skip the numbered instructions.

1. Hand each student a raisin box. Ask students not to open the box.

2. Begin the exercise in the same way that you did the mindful eating exercise involving the raisins, asking students to use their senses to explore the box.

3. Much as you did with the earlier exercise, ask students to slowly open the box and take out what they may find inside.

4. Invite students to explore with their senses what they have found.

5. Guide them through this so that they attend to the color of the tee, the sound of the tee as they tap it against the box, the feel of the tee, including its pointy tip. This is important because it will help to reinforce how they may subsequently use the tee as a mindfulness cue.

6. After completing this portion of the exercise, ask students to explain what they were experiencing from the moment you took out the boxes to give to each of them. You will find this to be a fun and lively discussion.

Distribute to students the full-color cards or your copies of the illustration and motion. Begin the illustration by asking students to take turns reading aloud, moving from top left to right as they work their way down the card, reading first what the tee is saying and then the caption. After each section is read, comment on how we all know and have a shared sense of these feelings.

After the illustration is read, turn to the Motion to Embrace. As you did with the illustration, have students take turns reading, beginning with the style of the case. This serves as a playful reminder to students of the ways that our brains are involved in this process. ("In the Neural Circuit Court"), and that uncertainty is a part of life and our discomfort arises when we resist reality ("You v. Reality"). As you then read through the motion itself, many important facts and insights are set forth, some of them reinforcing what you may have previously discussed in class. The motion concludes with an explicit and interactive demonstration of how the tee is a "mindfulness cue" that students can draw upon during challenging and stressful moments.

SUGGESTED TIMELINE
CLASS DEMONSTRATIONS, EXERCISES AND HOME PRACTICES

Pre-Class Assignment: "A Time I Didn't Stop" Questionnaire

Exercise:	Awareness of the Breath
Home Practice:	The Stop Sign

Exercise:	Awareness of the Breath
Home Practice:	The Pretextual Stop

Demonstration:	"The Snow Globe"
Exercise:	Awareness of the Breath (with Mindfulness Instruction)
Home Practice:	Notice the Snow Globe; Breath Awareness

Exercise:	Awareness of the Breath (with Mindfulness Instruction)
Home Practice:	"Stop Look & Listen" ("Just Is" Holmes)
Handout:	Judge-Mints

Demonstration:	"Ray of Zen"
Exercise:	Awareness of the Body
Home Practice:	Mindful Eating
Handout:	Judge-Mints

Discussion:	The Wandering Mind
Exercise:	Awareness of the Mind ("Just Is" Story)
Home Practice:	The Pre-Textual Stop
Handout:	"Landscape of the Mind" Illustration

Demonstration:	"The Spiral"
Exercise:	Awareness of the Breath
Home Practice:	The Spiral Illustration
Handout:	"The Spiral" Diagram

Discussion:	Practicing Mindfulness to De-Stress and to Cultivate Resilience
Exercise:	The Learned Hand "4–7–8" Hands Exercise
Home Practice:	"4–7–8 Hands" Exercise
Handout:	The "4–7–8 Hands" Reminder Card

The Mindfulness Immersion Class

Exercises:	Mindful Drinking
	Breath Awareness
	"Stop, Look & Listen"
	Mindful Walking
Handout:	Judge-Mints

Demonstration:	"Can You Spare a Dime?"
Exercise:	Select a Mindfulness Practice
Home Practice:	Designate Desired Number of Minutes (Dimes) To Sit
Handout:	"The Dime" Practice Reminder Card

Demonstration:	"The Motion to Embrace"
Exercise:	Motion to Embrace Life's Uncertain-Tees
Home Practice:	Embracing the Uncertain-Tee
Handout:	Some of Life's Uncertain-Tees Illustration and Tee

Exercise:	Four Prayers for Relief

CHAPTER 6:

MINDFUL ETHICS

*T*hus far we have shared with you a little of the history of mindfulness and the law, with a focus on its application to law students, of the contemplative practice of mindfulness, and of the integration of mindfulness into a law school classroom—namely, in a class that teaches professional responsibility. It is our hope that this material will be of assistance to you as you integrate mindfulness into your own class, regardless of what subject you may teach. Chapter 4 provides a big-picture perspective on how we went about this integration, and the more-detailed materials found both in that chapter and the various appendices are designed to provide you with specific approaches and materials which you can draw upon and apply in your class.

In this chapter we speak to an outcome of the class that we had not anticipated: a gestalt shift that seems to emerge out of the integration. And while this discussion is perhaps more fittingly explored as its own subject and in greater length elsewhere, we have decided to include it in this book so that those of you who are teaching mindfulness and professional responsibility can be sensitive to its expression in your own class, and so that together we might begin to assess its importance in the field of legal education. We have coined the phrase *mindful ethics* to begin this conversation.

Our collaboration and the integration of mindfulness and professional responsibility was the fortuitous coming together of what we happened to be teaching at the time. This specific integration resonated with us as a natural place to start, believing as we do that it offers an innovative way to teach professional responsibility while providing students with mindfulness tools that could be helpful in learning the curriculum and in practicing law. We recognized the natural synergy between the two areas, but did not think beyond it.

During the first few classes, we observed students grappling with the mindfulness practices while appreciating the connection to the professional responsibility material. For example, the Auto Awareness mindfulness exercises allow students to experience what it means to be aware of a rule that they may choose to break, thus directing a quality of meta-awareness to the experience. And because the Meeting of the Minds exercise encourages students to experience the vignettes from their own perspective, they were able to bring their personal exploration of mindfulness to the weekly assignments and classroom discussions. In this way, students begin to intuitively integrate the lessons to be learned from the classroom experience and homework assignments.

As the semester progressed and we watched the synergy between mindfulness and ethics take root, we experienced a bit of serendipity. Both of us sensed that something special was happening in the classroom. We saw it in the dynamics of the discussions that took place. Students were not only prepared in class, but they were also discussing the application of the rules with a heightened sensitivity to real-world applications and underlying policy concerns. Mindfulness was spilling into their comments about the rules, their views on the profession, and their personal goals and aspirations. Struggling with the rules that would regulate their conduct—and limit their freedom—students gave voice to their doubts about the sensibleness of rules, and they became viscerally engaged in discussing the application of the rules, personally,

> *Mindfulness and professionalism share a symbiotic relationship in the practice of law Mindfulness involves choosing to look at one's thoughts and to assess the contours and the weight those thoughts seem to have at any given moment, all without surrendering blindly to them. Through self-reflection, mindfulness creates a distance between the thought and belief in that thought. My sense is that that distance creates an opportunity for clarity and, ultimately (hopefully), wisdom. The practice of law, I suspect, will involve a great many questions and stressors that create tension. Mindfulness provides a way to mediate those tensions by providing an opportunity for the logic and principles of the rules and the conscience to resonate.*
>
> *—Cosme Caballero*
> *Spring 2011*

with regard to colleagues, and in relation to the representation of clients.

In so doing, students were living the rules, and in some cases exploring their own resolve to act in accordance with them, as well as considering and acknowledging their capacity to violate a rule. This latter consideration is the one that has the greatest gravity, and indeed, students recognized their capacity to want to resist a rule that they deemed "nonsensical" or "patronizing," as well as the possibility that in times of stress and confusion, they might traipse into dangerous territory. Students reported walking out of class with a heightened awareness that they possess a range of choices when they find themselves in challenging situations, along with a set of tools to help them navigate through this terrain. These shared insights led us to consider whether the integration might be taking on a life of its own. We have come to understand mindful ethics as the intuitive expression of meta-awareness into the process of ethical decision-making, much as if a Venn diagram of mindfulness and professional responsibility collapsed and the two areas merged into one circle.

> *There is no certainty that I will always make the most prudent decisions in my career and life; however, this class leaves me with the realization that, when I do make those decisions, it can be a deliberate exercise.*
>
> **—Gray Rivkin**
> *Fall 2011*

Why did this academic experiment produce this unexpected result? Mindful that hindsight is 20/20, we hesitate to explain why the integration of professional responsibility and mindfulness has had an impact that appears to be greater than the sum of its parts. Rather than delve too deeply at this nascent time, we look to your experience as you integrate this material so that a shared community of insight may emerge to document and explain this shift, and in so doing, advance the larger significance that it may play as a model to further enhance the quality of legal education. We have begun a blog to communicate our ongoing observations and encourage you to visit the Mindful Ethics blog at "www.mindfulethics.com and contribute your own.

APPLYING MINDFUL ETHICS ACROSS THE CURRICULUM

Legal educators such as Deborah Rhode have called for the integration of professional responsibility into the core curriculum, an approach that she terms *pervasive ethics*. If indeed mindful ethics embodies a qualitatively different experiencing of the rules and application of professional responsibility, then perhaps the integration of

> *The vignettes will stay in my mind because I know that I will be faced with many similar situations and one of the many things that I have learned from this course is to pause before you act and reflect on the thoughts, feelings, and sensations that you are experiencing to make a better decision in the future.*
>
> *—Sara Bradfield*
> *Spring 2011*

mindfulness and professional responsibility offers an exciting application of pervasive ethics in the classroom.

There are different ways to approach the incorporation of mindful ethics throughout the curriculum. One method involves selecting a case that does not contain an overt issue of professional responsibility and tweaking it to create a hypothetical discussion in much the same manner as the vignettes created for our class. In other words, the legal classroom is already a laboratory for hypothetically altering the facts of a case and analyzing factors that could change legal outcomes. Adjusting the facts to include an issue of professional responsibility as demonstrated by Deborah Rhode in pervasive ethics raises questions that open the door to a discussion of mindfulness.

> *As far as the rules go, I feel as though I learned them almost without realizing that I was learning them.*
>
> *— Jonathan Cohn*
> *Fall 2010*

Another approach, albeit one that does not lend itself to robust application, is to select a case that explicitly addresses ethical issues within a first-year class and integrating mindful ethics into the discussion. One obvious example in the area of tort law would be *Spaulding v. Zimmerman*, 263 Minn. 346 (1962).

Finally, professors who have a natural inclination and tendency toward creativity can develop vignettes in any area of the law by using the teaching tools discussed in chapter 4. An example is the vignette that has Pedro caught in the middle of his friend's crumbling marriage (see Appendix A, Vignette No. 4). The scenario is a typical one in the area of family law, although it is primarily focused on a conflict of interest and the mediation rules rather than substantive family law. The exploration of Pedro's feelings of loyalty, guilt, compassion, and so forth give rise to a discussion of mindfulness and the benefit to Pedro of developing the skills that allow for an awareness of his inner experience, so that his emotions do not compel him toward a regrettable decision.

The class teaches and practices methods which every lawyer, law-student, med-student, doctor, teacher, or anyone can use to cut through the chaos that has become part of daily life in our society. The recognition of the mindful self; the idea of looking inside to calm the storm, rather than looking for an external scapegoat; is a lesson that most students leave graduate school without. Mindfulness could be taught together with any subject, but its interplay with the rules of ethics provides an easy way for students to be introduced to a mindful practice. As law students, we learn the rules of ethics as a guide for how we should, and can, practice law. Students are looking outward for these rules as guideposts. The juxtaposition of these rules with mindfulness, looking inward for guideposts, for clarity, for understanding, provides a unique and inviting approach to the material.

—*Scott Rosen*
Spring 2012

Approaches like these provide the opportunity for students to more fully explore the components of decision-making and imagine how they might feel, as well as what their thoughts might be when challenged by an ethical dilemma. Students can contrast the reactivity of an impulsive decision with the thoughtful response resulting from the application of mindful awareness to the situation. Several students have told us that the role-playing aspect of our course greatly enhanced their learning experience. In fact, one of the students stated that after several weeks of working with the vignettes and the Meeting of the Minds journaling, he has begun imagining how he might feel and respond to cases while participating in other courses, finding that it assists him in his learning of the material.

The long-range impact of incorporating mindful ethics into the curriculum remains to be seen. However, early indications are that mindful ethics offers the promise and opportunity to instill in students a greater awareness of not only professionalism and the rules of conduct, but perhaps more importantly, of themselves and the tools with which they can achieve greater balance and ease in their lives.

RESOURCES

CHAPTER ONE: MINDFULNESS AND LEGAL EDUCATION

Books:

Daicoff, S., *Lawyer, Know Thyself* (APA, 2004).

Halpern, C., *Making Waves and Riding the Currents* (Berrett-Koehler, 2008).

Kauffman, G., *The Lawyer's Guide to Balancing Life & Work: Taking the Stress Out of Success* (ABA, 2006).

Keeva, S., *Transforming Practices: Finding Joy and Satisfaction in the Legal Life* (Contemporary Books, 1999).

Articles:

Allen, S., "Move From Being a Mindless Lawyer to a Mindful Lawyer," *The Complete Lawyer* (2008).

Cantrell, D., "A Compassionate Practice: Narratives from the Lives of Fifteen Buddhist Lawyers," 12 *Rutgers J. L. & Relig. 1* (2011).

Halpern, C., "The Mindful Lawyer: Why Contemporary Lawyers Are Practicing Meditation," 61 J. *Leg. Educ.* 641 (2011).

Hyman, J. P., "The Mindful Lawyer: Mindfulness Meditation and Law Practice," *Vermont Bar Journal.* (2007).

Krieger, L., "Add Human Nature As a New Guiding Philosophy for Legal Education and the Profession," 47 *Washurn L. J.* 247 (2008).

Magee, R., "Educating Lawyers to Meditate? From Exercises to Epistemology to Ethics: The Contemplative Practice and Law Movement as Legal Education Reform," 79 *UMKC L. Rev.* 535 (2011).

Riskin, L., "Awareness and the Legal Profession: An Introduction to the Mindful Lawyer Symposium," 61 J. *Leg. Educ.* 634 (2011).

Riskin, L.," Awareness in Lawyering: A Primer on Paying Attention," in *The Affective Assistance of Counsel: Practicing Law as a Healing Profession* 447-71 (Marjorie Silver, ed., Carolina Academic Press, 2007).

Riskin, L., "The Contemplative Lawyer: On the Potential Contributions of Mindfulness Meditation to Law Students, Lawyers, and their Clients," 7 *Harv. Negot. L. Rev* 1–66 (2002).

Rogers, S., "The Mindful Law School: An Integrative Approach to Transforming Legal Education" 28 *Touro L. Rev.* 1189 (2012).

Zeglovich, R. "The Mindful Lawyer," *GPSolo Magazine* (2006).

Websites:

http://mindfullawyerconference.org
http://contemplativelawstudents.com
http://contemplativelawyers.com
http://www.law.ufl.edu/imldr/index.shtml
http://mindfulness.law.miami.edu
http://themindfullawstudent.com
http://themindfullawprofessor.com
http://mindfulnessinlaw.com

CHAPTER TWO: MINDFULNESS: THE PRACTICE AND SCIENCE

Books:

Begley, S., *Train Your Mind, Change Your Brain: How a New Science Reveals Our Extraordinary Potential to Transform Ourselves* (Ballantine Books, 2007).

Goleman, D., *Social Intelligence: The New Science of Human Relationships* (Bantam Books, 2007).

Kabat-Zinn, J., *Coming to our Senses* (Hyperion, 2006).

Kabat-Zinn, J., *Mindfulness for Beginners: Reclaiming the Present Moment and Your Life* (Sounds True, Inc. 2012).

Kabat-Zinn, J., *Wherever You Go, There You Are* (Hyperion, 1994).

Langer, E., *Mindfulness* (De Capo Press, 1990).

Nhat Hanh, T., *The Miracle of Mindfulness: An Introduction to the Practice of Mindfulness* (Beacon Press 1999).

Ryan, T., *A Mindful Nation: How a Simple Practice Can Help Us Reduce Stress, Improve Performance, and Recapture the American Spirit* (Hay House Inc, 2012).

Shapiro, S., & Carlson, L., *The Art and Science of Mindfulness* (APA 2009).

Siegel, D., *The Mindful Brain: Reflection and Attunement in the Cultivation of Well-Being* (Norton 2006).

Smalley, S., & Winston, D., *Fully Present: The Science, Art and Practice of Mindfulness* (De Capo Press 2010).

Tan, C., *Search Inside Yourself: The Unexpected Path to Achieving Success, Happiness (and World Peace)* (Harper Collins 2012).

Articles:

Brown, K., & Ryan, R., "The Benefits of Being Present: Mindfulness and Its Role in Psychological Well-Being," 84 *J. Pers. & Soc. Psych.* 822, 822 (2003).

Holzel, B. K., Carmody, J., et. al., "Mindfulness Practice Leads to Increases in Regional Brain Gray Matter Density," *Psychiatry Res.* 191, 36–43 (2011).

Jha, A. P., Krompinger, J., et. al., "Mindfulness Training Modifies Subsystems of Attention," *Cogn. Affect. Behav. Neurosci.* 7,109–119 (2007).

Jha, A. P., et. al., "Examining the Protective Effects of Mindfulness Training on Working Memory and Affective Experience," *Emotion,* 10(1), 54–64. (2010).

Kabat Zinn, J., Davidson, R., et. al., "Alterations in Brain and Immune Function Produced by Mindfulness Meditation," *Psychosomatic Medicine* 65:564-570 (2003).

Lazar, S., et. al., "Meditation Experience is Associated with Increased Cortical Thickness," *NeuroReport,* 16: 1893–1897 (2005).

Luders, E., Toga, A. W. et. al., "The Underlying Anatomical Correlates of Long-term Meditation: Larger Hippocampal and Frontal Volumes of Gray Matter," *Neuroimage* 45, 672–678 (2009).

Luders, E., Clark, K., et.al., "Enhanced Brain Connectivity in Long-term Meditation Practitioners," *Neuroimage* 57, 1308–1316 (2011).

Luders, E., Kurth, F., et. al., "The Unique Brain Anatomy of Meditation Practitioners: Alterations in Cortical Gyrification," *Frontiers in Human Neuroscience,* 6:1–9 (2012).

Riskin, L., "The Contemplative Lawyer: On the Potential Contributions of Mindfulness Meditation to Law Students, Lawyers, and their Clients," 7 *Harvard Negotiation Law Review* 1–66 (2002).

Websites:

http://marc.ucla.edu
http://mindandlife.org

http://psyphz.psych.wisc.edu/
http://spiritrock.org
http://www.umassmed.edu/cfm

CHAPTER THREE: MINDFULNESS AND THE LAW SCHOOL CURRICULUM

Books:

Langer, E., *The Power of Mindful Learning* (Perseus 1997).

Rogers, S., *Mindfulness for Law Students: Applying the Power of Mindfulness to Achieve Balance and Success in Law School* (Mindful Living Press 2009).

Schoeberlein, D., *Mindful Teaching and Teaching Mindfulness: A Guide for Anyone Who Teaches Anything* (Wisdom Publications 2009).

Articles:

Alfieri, A., "Educating Lawyers for Community" (January 24, 2012). Wisconsin Law Review, 2012; University of Miami Legal Studies Research Paper No. 2012–02.

Lerner, A., "Using Our Brains: What Cognitive Science and Social Psychology Teach Us About Teaching Law Students to Make Ethical, Professionally Responsible, Choices," 23 *Quinnipiac L. Rev.* 643 (2004).

Magee, R., "Educating Lawyers to Meditate? From Exercises to Epistemology to Ethics: The Contemplative Practice and Law Movement as Legal Education Reform," 79 *UMKC L. Rev.* 535 (2011).

Magee, R., "Mindfulness and the Renewal of Legal Education, New Directions for Teaching and Learning," (Josey Bass, forthcoming 2012).

Riskin, L., "Awareness in Lawyering: A Primer on Paying Attention," in *The Affective Assistance of Counsel: Practicing Law as a Healing Profession* 447–71 (Marjorie Silver, ed., Carolina Academic Press, 2007).

Rogers, S., "Experiencing Grade Anxiety: Mindfulness Offers Clarity," *Res Ipsa Loquitur*, 15 (UM Law School, February 2009).

Rogers, S., "Opinion: Managing Law School Stress," *Res Ipsa Loquitur,* 15 (UM Law School, March–April 2009).

Reuben, R., "Bringing Mindfulness into the Classroom: A Personal Journey," 61 *J. Leg. Educ.* 674 (2011).

Zlotnick, D., "Integrating Mindfulness Theory and Practice into Trial Advocacy," 61 *J. Leg. Educ.* 654 (2011).

Websites:

http://www.law.berkeley.edu/mindfulness.htm
http://mindfulethics.com
http://mindfulness.law.miami.edu
http://themindfulclassroom.com
http://themindfullawstudent.com

CHAPTER FOUR: INTEGRATING MINDFULNESS AND PROFESSIONAL RESPONSIBILITY

Books:

Rogers, S., *Mindfulness for Law Students: Applying the Power of Mindfulness to Achieve Balance and Success in Law School* (Mindful Living Press 2009).

Articles:

Gold, A., "Mindfulness: A Challenge for Our Times," *Dade-County Bar Association Bulletin,* (May 2012).

Magee, R., "Educating Lawyers to Meditate? From Exercises to Epistemology to Ethics: The Contemplative Practice and Law Movement as Legal Education Reform," 79 *UMKC L. Rev.* 535 (2011).

Riskin, L., "Awareness and Ethics in Dispute Resolution and Law: Why Mindfulness Tends to Foster Ethical Behavior," *S. Tex. L. Rev.* 493–503 (2009).

Ruedy, N., Schweitzer, M., "In the Moment: The Effect of Mindfulness on Ethical Decision Making" 95 *J. Bus. Ethics* 73 (2010).

Websites:

http://mindfulethics.com
http://www.buffalo.edu/news/11656

CHAPTER FIVE: MINDFULNESS DEMONSTRATIONS & EXERCISES FOR THE LAW SCHOOL CLASSROOM

Books:

Rogers, S., *Mindfulness for Law Students: Using the Power of Mindful Awareness to Achieve Balance and Success in Law School* (Mindful Living Press 2009).

Articles:

Calloway, D., "Using Mindfulness Practice to Work with Emotions," 10 *Nev. L. Rev.* 338 (2010).

Cantrell, D., "The Role of Equipoise in Family Law," 13 *J. L. & Fam. Stud.* 63 (2012).

Larkin-Wong, K., "A Newbie's Impression: One Student's Mindfulness Lessons," 61 *J. Leg. Educ.* 665 (2011).

Magee, R., "Educating Lawyers to Meditate? From Exercises to Epistemology to Ethics: The Contemplative Practice and Law Movement as Legal Education Reform," 79 *UMKC L. Rev.* 535 (2011).

Rogers, S., "Stop, Look & Listen—Regain Your Focus Through Mindfulness," ABA: *The Young Lawyer,* Volume 15, Number 4, February 2011.

Websites:

http://themindfulclassroom.com
http://themindfullawprofessor.com
http://themindfullawstudent.com

CHAPTER SIX: MINDFUL ETHICS

Books:

Davidson, R and Begley, S., *The Emotional Life of Your Brain: How Its Unique Patterns Affect the Way You Think, Feel, and Live–and How You Can Change Them* (Penguin 2012).

Langer, E., *The Power of Mindful Learning* (Perseus 1997).

Lehrer, L., *How We Decide* (Houghton Mifflin Co. 2009).

Rhode, D., *Professional Responsibility: Ethics by the Pervasive Method* (Aspen Publishers 1998).

Articles:

Harris, A., "Toward Lawyering as Peacemaking: A Seminar on Mindfulness, Morality, and Professional Identity," 61 *J. Leg. Educ.* 647 (2011).

Krieger, L., "The Most Ethical of People, the Least Ethical of People: Proposing Self-Determination Theory to Measure Professional Character Formation," 8 *U. St. Thomas L.J.* 168 (2011).

Lerner, A., "Using Our Brains: What Cognitive Science and Social Psychology Teach us About Teaching Law Students to Make Ethical, Professionally Responsible, Choices," 23 *Quinnipiac L. Rev.* 643 (2004).

Magee, R., "Educating Lawyers to Meditate? From Exercises to Epistemology to Ethics: The Contemplative Practice and Law Movement as Legal Education Reform," 79 *UMKC L. Rev.* 535 (2011).

Peppet, S., "Can Saints Negotiate? A Brief Introduction to Problems of Imperfect Ethics in Bargaining," 7 *Harv. Negot. L. Rev.* 87 (2002).

Riskin, L., "Awareness and Ethics in Dispute Resolution and Law: Why Mindfulness Tends to Foster Ethical Behavior," 50 *S. Tex. L. Rev.* 493-503 (2009).

Ruedy, N., Schweitzer, M., "In the Moment: The Effect of Mindfulness on Ethical Decision Making" 95 *J. Bus. Ethics* 93 (2010).

Shapiro, S. L., Jazaieri, H., & Goldin, P. R., "Mindfulness-Based Stress Reduction Effects on Moral Reasoning and Decision Making," (Unpublished manuscript 2012).

Websites:

http://mindfulethics.com
http://mindfullawyerconference.org
http://www.law.ufl.edu/imldr/index.shtml

APPENDIX A

CLASS VIGNETTES

*B*y developing the primary course material ourselves, we were able to assign readings and focus the homework and classroom discussion on professional responsibility issues that naturally connected with mindfulness themes. The Vignettes, as discussed more completely in chapter 4, were the basis for both the student's analysis and application of the rules of professional responsibility (the "Vignette Analysis Form"), as well as the mindfulness journaling exercise (the "Meeting of the Minds").

We have included in this appendix a sampling of these materials to provide you with examples of this approach. These vignettes have been selected as representative of the course material while also giving you a sense of how the Pedro and Mindy story line follows their legal careers. We begin this Appendix with the first assignment students complete prior to the first day of class, "A Time I Didn't Stop."

You may visit the website www.mindfulethics.com/the-book.html to view all of the vignettes along with links to the rules and readings.

111

FIRST CLASS ASSIGNMENT (ANONYMOUS)

Dear Class:

The legal profession is self-regulating. The American Bar Association has developed model rules to govern attorney conduct and the states each enact their own rules using the model rules as a guideline. The various State Bar Associations issue advisory opinions as well as decisions based upon disciplinary hearings. Thus, an attorney may consult these rules and opinions, other treatises, and usually there is also a state bar "hotline" to call or website to consult if there is any question as to what behavior is appropriate and permissible.

So, it may be hard to imagine that with all these resources available, attorneys (sometimes well-respected attorneys) continue to violate these rules knowing that they are doing so, but unable to muster the capacity to allow their better judgment to call the shots. Why? This is something that we will be exploring together this semester, as we review, with a heightened level of awareness, the rules of professional conduct in the social media context.

Your first assignment is to recall a time in your life when you engaged in conduct that you knew was improper, but did so anyway. In the fields below, please write a paragraph recollecting this moment. Give thought as to why you think that you did what you did even though you knew better, and include this insight in your discussion.

Your responses are anonymous but may be used for classroom discussion.

"A Time I Didn't Stop"

Recall a time in your life when you engaged in conduct that you knew was improper, but did so anyway.

_____

_____

_____

_____

_____

Share your insights into why you think you did this even though "you knew better."

_____

_____

_____

_____

THE FIRST VIGNETTE

Professional Responsibility Themes:

The course begins with an immersion into the rules of professional responsibility in the first vignette, which is set in the context of a large law firm. Our characters, Pedro and Mindy, are employed as associates. Pedro is a new associate and his assignment to a large case provides the vehicle to not only explore the fundamental rules of competence, diligence, communication and confidentiality, but also introduces the rules pertaining to relationships with colleagues, clients, opposing counsel, and the court.

"THE ROAD TO DISCOVERY – DOCUMENTS AND YOURSELF"

This week we are introduced to two young lawyers whose legal careers we will follow over the course of the semester. Mindy Fuller is a third year associate at a large law firm. Pedro Respono has just joined the firm. Pedro's journey begins with his first big case and the various ethical questions that emerge as he makes his way through this exciting and challenging time in his career.

* * *

Pedro Respono is excited and nervous to begin work as an associate at the big firm. He had clerked at the firm one summer and enjoyed several prestigious judicial clerkships after graduating law school. But today marks the start of his real career. He is assigned to the litigation team working on a major commercial case that involves a patent dispute concerning the ownership of new cutting-edge technology. Mindy Fuller, a third-year associate that Pedro had known in law school, tells Pedro that it is a great assignment because he will be working with Laura, one of the firm's most ambitious young partners, and Larry, one of the firm's most experienced paralegals.

The case is currently in discovery and Pedro is assigned to review the pleadings so that he can assist with the document review and deposition preparation. As Pedro reviews the documents produced by the opposing party, he finds a disk with documents that appear to be inadvertently produced; there are letters between the opposing attorney and his client discussing the case strategy and possible witnesses. Unsure of what to do, Pedro takes the disk to Laura. She begins taking copious notes and then thanks him for being so thorough.

Later that week, Pedro asks Larry, who is cataloging the new documents, whether there is anything wrong with using them since they seem to have been accidentally produced. Larry comments that it's not the firm's fault that the other side might have produced the wrong documents. Sensing that Pedro was still doubtful, he reassures him that there are new ethical rules that don't require a lawyer to return inadvertently produced documents. "Don't worry about it," he tells Pedro. Larry changes the conversation, showing Pedro how he is using Facebook to "friend" as many of the other side's witnesses as possible to gather additional information for depositions and cross examination.

Pedro decides to focus his energy on doing the best job he can to assist Laura in preparing the firm's client's employees for their depositions. He accompanies Laura to prepare the main witnesses and impresses her with his knowledge of the case. She allows Pedro to prepare one of the minor witnesses while she observes. Laura tells Pedro that he has done a great job and asks him to prepare other witnesses on his own with Larry assisting the process.

Pedro works late into the night studying the case and the documents that he needs to review with his first witness. He prepares mock questions to ask the witness so that not only will the witness be prepared, but also Pedro will be sharpening his skills in hopes of being able to take a deposition of one of the opposing party's witnesses.

The next day, Pedro meets with Claire, an employee of the client who is on the witness list. Pedro carefully reviews all of the documents with her and asks her questions as if he is the opposing counsel. Pedro's thoroughness results in Claire discussing documents with which Pedro is unfamiliar. She shows Pedro 21 emails that appear to be relevant to the discovery requests, but had not been produced. Pedro wonders whether the keywords used to do the electronic discovery search were adequate to cover these emails.

Pedro reports to Laura on his meeting with Claire and informs her and Larry of the additional emails, showing them copies. Laura looks at the first several documents and explains that they either are not responsive to the way the discovery request was framed or privileged.

While Pedro is unsure about Laura's decision, he feels comforted that he raised it with her and reminds himself that just because he might decide differently doesn't mean that he's right. Pedro is excited about the prospect of participating as third chair at the trial, defined as "the learning seat." He is there to take notes, run errands and absorb as much as possible. Pedro is ecstatic! This is why he attended law school---Pedro updates his friends on Facebook every evening as to the happenings at the trial. He has also started a young lawyer's blog on which he describes the trial. The trial appears to be going well for his client.

Unfortunately, midway through the trial, Pedro's dream seems to be turning into a nightmare. Laura demolished a witness during cross-examination using notes she had taken from the inadvertently produced documents and the information that Larry had obtained from the Facebook witnesses. Opposing counsel is outraged and moves to disqualify the firm. The client is confused and upset. Furthermore, on cross-examination Claire referred to the 21 emails that had not been produced. When asked whether she had discussed them with any of her lawyers, Laura raises the attorney-client privilege. The Judge is losing his patience and orders the firm to revisit the electronic search. Pedro looks over the original discovery request and realizes that the e-mails were clearly responsive. When appropriate keywords are entered, the search reveals an additional 46,000 documents that should have been produced.

The Judge disqualifies the firm from representing the client based on Laura's use of the information from the inadvertently produced documents, sanctions Laura for the discovery violations, and refers her to the state bar. She resigns from the firm in disgrace. The Judge calls Pedro aside during a recess, and tells him that he narrowly escaped being reported to the Bar. Pedro silently recollects his conversations with Claire when she told him about the 21 documents and nods.

A few months later, during Pedro's annual review, the managing partner tells him that he was extremely disappointed with his handling of the discovery matters in the case and his failure to speak with someone other than Laura and Larry at the firm. The partner says that the firm's reputation is all the more important during tough economic times and the firm has decided to terminate Pedro's employment. Pedro feels sick and disillusioned as he ponders the events and his future.

THE SECOND VIGNETTE

Professional Responsibility Themes:

Pedro's foray into solo practice and his use of outsourcing, listservs, and blogging is the vehicle for debating outsourcing and exploring the use of technology and social media in the practice of law. Outsourcing, a cutting edge issue, provides a wonderful way to revisit the fundamental rules of competence, diligence, communication and confidentiality, while introducing the concepts of conflict of interest and the unauthorized practice of law.

"OUTSOURCING EVERYTHING BUT YOUR LICENSE"

Having been asked to leave the firm, Pedro considers various options and decides to go solo and hang out his shingle. He has a few clients who appreciate the reduced fees and extra attention. Mindy, a loyal friend through it all is excited for Pedro and remains in close contact with him.

* * *

Pedro continues to share his career thoughts and feelings on his blog and others often join the discussion. The blog continues to be a source of support and encouragement for Pedro in his new venture. However, support and encouragement do not pay the bills, so Pedro commits himself to increasing his book of business.

Friends begin to look to Pedro for help with small matters and old friendships begin to lead to promising clients. One day while Pedro is having lunch with Derrick, a college roommate and good friend, Derrick mentions that his wife, Samantha, has decided to start her own business. She needs assistance with forming a corporation and will need representation with other legal matters. Pedro excitedly offers to help, noting that he had drafted and filed incorporation documents while servicing some of the firm's smaller clients. He meets with Samantha and she becomes his first corporate client. He incorporates her company and she calls him regularly for basic legal advice.

Although Pedro feels fortunate that his friends and colleagues are sending him business, he is also frustrated because of the missed opportunities for

---

additional business; he has turned away potential clients because he felt that the work was over his head. He begins to take CLE classes to learn new areas of the law hoping that he will not have to turn anyone else away.

One day someone from his former firm, remembering that Pedro worked on a big patent case, refers a client to Pedro because the firm has a conflict. The client has a new matter that is likely to be huge.

This is a great opportunity for Pedro; however, he really doesn't know much about patent law and he does not have any staff to assist him. That big case is just a blur now and most of the work he did was not substantive in nature. Pedro has signed up for a solo practitioner "listeserv" named MYSHINGLE and asks the group whether he should accept the case. An attorney responds, "Are you serious? You can figure out how to handle any case. Why would you throw away all that money?"

Pedro posts his dilemma on his blog, "P.R. Blawg" and someone suggests that Pedro use outsourcing to solve his problem. Pedro does some research and learns that there is a company in India that can do any aspect of a case for you. He reads a testimonial about the company and is sold. He is ecstatic! Pedro accepts the client's case and outsources much of the legal work to LegalAssist, the company in India.

LegalAssist conducts the necessary research and prepares the pleadings. Pedro studies the motion for summary judgment provided by LegalAssist and is able to win the case for the client. Pedro bills the client at Pedro's regular rate, which is much less than the large firm, and the client is thrilled. Pedro has his overhead covered and has learned another way to use the digital age to succeed.

THE THIRD VIGNETTE

Professional Responsibility Themes:

Mindy's decision to join Pedro in solo practice and share his office space sets the stage for an exploration of the rules regarding trust accounts, signage and the advantages and cautions of sharing office space. Confidentiality is revisited in several contexts and the issues arising in a virtual law practice are introduced.

"AVATARS AND ADMINISTRATION: SECOND LIFE, SECOND GUESSING, AND SECOND CHANCES"

After four years with the law firm, Mindy decides to resign. She is tired of the long hours she spends working on other attorneys' cases, which leaves her little time for a life, let alone client development. Overall, the four years at the firm have been worthwhile, but the time is right to move on. She also has one firm client who is so happy with Mindy's work that he wants Mindy to handle his future legal needs. Having kept up with Pedro and his growing success, not to mention the freedom he has gained by practicing on his own, Mindy gives serious thought to going solo. She has saved some money, which will help her seed a solo practice and has good experience. She speaks with Pedro and they decide that Mindy will share office space, which will be cost effective for both of them. Plus, they will be able to bounce ideas off of each other and brainstorm together.

* * *

Shortly after moving into her office, Mindy begins to focus on the administrative aspects of starting a law office. She incorporates as Mindy Fuller, P.A. and literally places a shingle on the wall outside the office's front door. She opens a business account at a nearby bank, and deposits $5,000 of her personal funds to establish the account with enough liquidity for the next several months' expenses.

When she returns to her office, Mindy notices the one large client file that she brought from the firm. Pedro comes into Mindy's office to ask if she needs anything. Mindy looks at the client file in her hand and says, "I guess I'll need some file cabinets." Pedro tells Mindy that she can share the bottom drawer of one of his file cabinets until she has more clients and wants to buy her own. Together they walk into his office and he pulls open the bottom drawer of the cabinet. Mindy pauses to consider the propriety of sharing the drawer.

"Come on" Pedro laughs. "It's just a drawer. It's not going to slam shut on you." Mindy inserts the file, remembering to take from it the $5,000 retainer check that the client sent to fund future work. Mindy grabs one of the new Business Checking deposit slips for her P.A. and fills it out to deposit the retainer. She drops it in the night deposit box on her way home that evening.

A few days later, Mindy calls the web-design firm that her former firm uses. She has a good relationship with the owner and he agrees to give her a great deal on a website and two month's Internet marketing to send "eyeballs" to the website. Excited to get the ball rolling, since all she has is the Caado profile, Mindy writes a $1,000 check for the design and marketing services and places it in the mail. Asked if she also needs general marketing, Mindy says that she has some ideas, which she can implement herself. Mindy has been a Second Life junky for over a year and finally sees a way to turn it into a business development tool.

Mindy logs on to "Second Life" and sets up the avatar "Lawfirm Solo." She plans to use the avatar as a way to generate business and the "Second Life" service as a forum for advertising her services. To start the ball rolling, she runs the ad:

"Lawfirm Solo: Expert Answers to Your Second Life and Real Life Legal Questions. Receive a Two Paragraph Answer for 1000 Linden Dollars. Not into Relationships, Even "Attorney-Client." Just a Short Q and A to Get You On Your Way."

Although Mindy is unsure how effective the ad will be, later that afternoon an SL user contacts Mindy and asks a virtual world legal question. Mindy answers it. $1000 Linden appears in her Second Life account.

Excited with her first piece of business as a solo practitioner, Mindy gets together with her best friend, Claudia, to celebrate. Over dinner, Mindy tells Claudia about her new Second Life client and the interesting legal question that was raised.

THE FOURTH VIGNETTE

Professional Responsibility Themes:

The marital difficulties of Pedro's friends, who are characters previously introduced to the students, reflect Pedro's conflicts of interest from both a personal and professional standpoint. Obligations to prospective, current and former clients along with the ethics of mediation are the basis of this vignette.

"CONFLICTS AND CONFIDENCES: THE MINDFUL PATH TO CLARITY AND COURAGE"

One day while having breakfast with Derrick, Pedro learns that Derrick and Samantha are going through a rough time. Derrick shares that Samantha's business is extremely successful, but she is never home and they have grown apart. Pedro sympathizes, offering him words of comfort. As they leave, Derrick asks if he can count on Pedro's support and help, to which Pedro replies, "Of course."

The next week Derrick calls to explain that he read one of Samantha's e-mails to her best friend and learned that she is planning on getting an attorney to file for divorce. Derrick is clearly upset and says that he wants to file first. He asks Pedro to file whatever is necessary so that Samantha doesn't get the upper hand. Pedro replies that he is not sure that it is a good idea for him to get in the middle of the case since he is a friend of both Derrick and Samantha.

Derrick bemoans his situation and pleads for Pedro to represent him, saying that he thought Pedro had agreed when they last met for lunch. Also, Derrick confides, that he trusts no one, but Pedro. Derrick begins to break down as he shares his sadness over the prospect of getting divorced and Pedro relents, agreeing to represent Derrick on the condition that the situation "remains cordial." Pedro says, in a serious tone, that if Derrick decides that he wants a bulldog, then he will have to retain someone else. Derrick agrees and expresses his gratitude.

That afternoon, Pedro receives a call from Samantha who says that she is planning to divorce Derrick. She requests an appointment with Pedro and a recommendation for a competent family law lawyer. She says that she would not ask Pedro to represent her because he and Derrick are such good friends.

Pedro says that he is uncomfortable providing a recommendation. Samantha becomes irritated saying that she only wants to meet to discuss lawyer options and nothing else. Pedro apologizes, but remains firm.

Samantha exclaims, "You have been my lawyer for years. I have paid and confided in you. You are not going to abandon me now. I trust you and only you."

Her voice becomes so loud that Pedro has to move the phone away from his ear. Pedro responds: "I need to think it through and will call you back."

Pedro discusses the matter with Mindy, who suggests that Pedro may have an attorney-client relationship with Samantha that precludes his representation of Derrick.

Pedro calls Derrick and explains, "I would really love to help you, but because I have represented Samantha, it could create a messy situation."

A dejected Derrick laments his woes on the phone and in the ensuing silence Pedro comes up with an idea. "How about this," he says. "I am a certified mediator in family law. If Samantha is game, I will try to mediate your divorce. We can all get together and try to work out the terms." Derrick agrees and says he'll ask Samantha..

Vignette Analysis Form

Name _____

What is the Professional Responsibility "Event"?	What rule(s) may be implicated?	Was there a violation of the rule(s)?	Why or why not?	Do you agree?	What was the "Want"?
		1---2---3---4---5 No Yes		No : Yes	
		1---2---3---4---5		No : Yes	
		1---2---3---4---5		No : Yes	
		1---2---3---4---5		No : Yes	

APPENDIX B

MINDFULNESS HANDOUTS

*M*indfulness demonstrations and exercises, and the insights and inspiration that flow from them, can be reinforced through the distribution of materials that reinforce them. The Institute for Mindfulness Studies has developed a collection of handouts that we use in our class and which are made available for your use, pursuant to the terms provided.

These handouts, comprised of illustrations, motions, and cues, are reproduced in this Appendix. Below you will find an outline of these materials. A brief discussion of the illustrations and motions follows, with a fuller discussion provided for those motions that are not discussed in the body of this book.

The mindfulness cues, many of which you may order from the Institute for Mindfulness Studies, either separately or as a class set, are pictured and described so that that you may better glimpse how they support a meaningful and engaging class demonstration or exercise.

Illustrations
Landscape of the Mind
The Spiral
Some of Life's Uncertain-Tees

Motions
Motion to Embrace
Motion to Recuse
Motion for Extension of Time
Motion for Relief from Judgment

Mindfulness Cues
Can You Spare a Dime?
Judge-Mints
Extension of Thyme
Uncertain-Tee
"4–7–8" Learned Hand Exercise Card
"Just Is" Holmes Exercise Card

ILLUSTRATIONS

Landscape of the Mind

The Landscape of the Mind illustration facilitates a discussion of the "wandering mind" and how our tendency to become distracted can take us to counterproductive places (see pages 130 & 131); see also *Mindfulness for Law Students,* at page 34.

The Spiral

Discussed more fully on page 52, this diagram serves as a mindfulness tool for students to reflect on after "The Spiral" demonstration. As a take-home exercise students are asked to fill in the diagram when they experience a challenging or difficult event. It is helpful for bringing greater awareness to stressful situations, and to learning how to identify and notice thoughts, feelings, and body sensations, along with the ways we can overreact.

Some of Life's Uncertain-Tees

This illustration, which accompanies the Motion to Embrace demonstration (see page 91) offers a humorous look into the adventures of a golf tee that undergoes a series of unsettling experiences, provoking the everyday distress all too familiar to the human condition.

THE MOTIONS

Motion to Recuse

This motion is one that offers students insight into the judgmental nature of their minds and the ways such a critical edge can, at times, prove counterproductive and even destructive. The motion can be used to explore the distinction between "judgment" as a defensive, reactive force and a Solomon-like "judgment" that is imbued with wisdom and compassion. As such the motion can serve as a vehicle to explore the meaning of "non-judgmental awareness." In class, we discuss the pros

126

and cons of granting such a motion, and suggest that it is best taken under advisement.

Motion to Embrace (Life's Uncertain-Tees)

This motion (and the accompanying illustration) offer a creative way to sum up the mindfulness insights explored over the course of the semester and provide an exercise, and mindfulness cue, that students may use in their daily life.

Motion for Extension of Time (and Order Granting Extension)

The *Motion for Extension of Time,* which is not discussed in the body of the book, offers a mindfulness insight (and accompanying cue) and can be introduced in class to support a number of important lessons connected to the challenges occasioned by time, such as feelings of urgency, missing or feeling overwhelmed with deadlines, and procrastination.

As one example, you can explore with students the common experience of falling behind on a project and the ways that we can make mistakes through the stress of feeling that there is not enough time. This discussion naturally leads the mindfulness insight that thoughts and feelings and the stress of "not enough time" might be reactive, and that, in fact, there may be enough time were we to be able to focus, or, even if there is not adequate time, the worst case scenario we are dreading is not likely to occur. The *Motion for Extension of Time* can then be distributed and read aloud, inviting students to fill in the blanks at the end of the respective sentences.

After reviewing some of their responses, surprise them by telling them you will grant their motion. Distribute to each student a sprig of thyme—literally an "extension of thyme." You can find sprigs of thyme at your local grocery store. Use the aroma, as a mindfulness practice of paying attention, i.e., coming to our senses. The *Order Granting Extension of Thyme* can then be given to students afterward to reinforce this cue.

127

Motion for Relief from Judgment (and Order Granting Relief)

The *Motion for Relief from Judgment* offers insight into the ways that our judgmental nature can lead to suffering. The *Order Granting Relief from Judgment* is a reminder that a mindfulness practice is a vehicle to find relief from suffering by working with reactivity, finding a deeply felt sense of relief, and a better way of relating to unwanted events, challenging people, and difficult situations.

ILLUSTRATIONS

131

"The Spiral"

_____

_____

_____

_____

"The Event"

Thoughts

S R

F

T

Feelings

_____

_____

_____

**(Over-)
Reactions**

**Body
Sensations**

_____

_____

_____

Observations

_____

_____

_____

Some of Life's Uncertain-Tees™

"Self Doubt"

"Things not working out as planned"

"People getting upset or disapproving"

"Rejection"

"Fear"

"Will it ever end?"

MOTIONS

IN THE NEURAL CIRCUIT COURT IN AND FOR
THE GREAT AND HEALTHY STATE OF MIND

YOU, aka "ME"

                Petitioner,

      vs.

REALITY,

                Respondent.

_____/

MOTION TO EMBRACE LIFE'S UNCERTAINTIES

Pursuant to the laws of the great and healthy State of Mind, Petitioner respectfully moves this neural circuit court for **relief from judgment** so that Petitioner may **embrace life's uncertainties with optimism and courage.**

1. Judging the Future: In an effort to survive, an over zealous "Me" will occasionally prejudge the future. These judgments are almost always **fear-based,** and as such, anticipate worst case scenarios that become a source of anxiety and worry.

2. The Wandering Mind: As these judgments about the future proliferate, thinking becomes scattered and it is difficult to stay on track and attend to work, family, and friends with focus, clarity, and compassion.

3. The Afflicted Body: This mental activity takes its toll on the brain and body as memory becomes impaired, the cardiovascular system is taxed, and immune functioning deteriorates.

4. Mindfulness: Psychologists and neuroscientists are finding that "uncertainty" is not the source of alarm, but rather, how Petitioner relates to uncertainty. Mindfulness invites Petitioner to **move toward the discomfort** by embracing life's forever uncertain nature.

5. Neuroscience: Neuroscientists and psychologists are finding that by embracing the discomfort that arises amid life's uncertainties, mind and body move into **greater balance and integration.**

6. Practice: Petitioner can embrace life's uncertainties with **optimism and courage** by:

   a. Placing the Tee, attached as Exhibit "A," in plain view on their desk.
   b. During challenging moments of uncertainty, allowing the Tee to serve as a reminder that worrisome thoughts and feelings are momentary activities of the mind and body that arise and pass away.
   c. Slowly reaching out a hand and embracing the "Uncertain-Tee," as a **reminder** that the discomfort is bearable.
   d. "Seeing" the color of the Tee, "feeling" its texture, and exploring other **sensory experiences** like sound, taste, and smell, thereby quieting the mind.
   e. **Breathing.** Bringing awareness to your beating heart. Smiling.

WHEREFORE, for the reasons set forth above, the **Motion to Embrace** should be granted.

Respectfully submitted,

_____

Me

IN THE NEURAL CIRCUIT COURT IN AND FOR
THE GREAT AND HEALTHY STATE OF MIND

YOU, aka "ME"

Petitioner,

vs.

REALITY

Respondent.

_____/

MOTION TO RECUSE

Pursuant to the laws of the great and healthy State of Mind, Petitioner respectfully moves for the recusal of Petitioner **as judge** over these proceedings. For the reasons set forth below, Judge You should be recused from these proceedings.

1. No Accountability: Judge You was not elected, was not appointed, and was not even confirmed with the advice and consent of anyone.

2. No Experience: Judge You had no prior experience. He didn't even have all of his brain cells when he took the bench.

3. Conflict of Interest: Judge You has multiple conflicts of interest. These include, *inter alia:*

   a. He has a personal bias against the Respondent, Reality, when it does not go his way.
   b. He has been known to deny Reality without giving it an opportunity to be heard.

4. Lack of Jurisidiction: Notwithstanding that the jurisdictional limits of Judge You's authority is his own life, he continues to judge everybody else's life.

5. Ex Parte Communications: Judge You continues to engage in ex parte communications with himself. Judge You is constantly issuing Temporary Restraining Orders seeking to maintain the status quo.

6. Improper Use of Interpreter: When the Court has required the use of an interpreter to clarify and explain past events, Judge You has appointed himself to serve as interpreter and provided a biased and partial interpretation of events and witnesses statements.

Prejudgment of Facts and Law: Judge You has a need to be right and for others to be wrong. In addition, he prejudges facts, witnesses, and the law. Judge You has his own preferences for the laws of nature and, when Reality does not go his way, he becomes angry, frustrated, and resists accepting it. On occasions, Judge You is so resistant to reality that he is afraid to rule on pending motions and, as a result, has an overwhelming docket.

Double Bias: The only argument advanced in opposition to recusal is that Judge You is often harsh, judgmental, doubtful, and critical of himself. This, too, however, supports a finding of bias. Clearly, this is not a judge who has a balanced and even judicial temperament over matters involving his life, liberty, or pursuit of happiness.

WHEREFORE, for the reasons set forth above, the **Motion to Rescue** [sic] should be granted.

Respectfully submitted,

_____

You, Esq.
Counsel for Petitioner

IN THE NEURAL CIRCUIT COURT IN AND FOR
THE GREAT AND HEALTHY STATE OF MIND

YOU, aka "ME"

          Petitioner,

    vs.

REALITY

          Respondent.

_____/

MOTION FOR EXTENSION OF TIME

Pursuant to the laws of the great and healthy State of Mind, Petitioner respectfully moves for an order extending the amount of time available to focus on law school studies and related tasks and projects.

1. Petitioner is enrolled in law school, known far and wide as a grueling experience where time is short and the workload is heavy.

2. From time to time, Petitioner finds that there is not enough time to get everything done. Such times include:

_____.

3. During such times, Petitioner begins to think that:

_____.

4. Petitioner feels:

_____.

5. Petitioner also experiences sensations in the body that include:

_____.

6. As a result, Petitioner occasionally feels a sense of urgency that increases stress, undermines Petitioner's ability to perform optimally, and adversely affects Petitioner's relationship with:

_____.

WHEREFORE, Petitioner respectfully requests that this Court enter an order extending the amount of time Petitioner has to study for class, prepare for exams, finish projects, exercise, eat, relax, sleep, and spend time with friends and family.

Respectfully submitted,

_____

YOU, Esq.

IN THE NEURAL CIRCUIT COURT IN AND FOR
THE GREAT AND HEALTHY STATE OF MIND

YOU, aka "ME"

           Petitioner,

      vs.

REALITY

           Respondent.

_____/

ORDER GRANTING EXTENSION OF THYME

Before this Neural Circuit Court is Petitioner's Motion for Extension of Time. For the reasons set forth below, Petitioner's Motion is GRANTED.

1. This Court finds that Petitioner is enrolled in law school, which can be a grueling experience in which there is limited time to accomplish a great deal. This Court also finds that there are moments when Petitioner believes that there is not enough time to get everything done. During moments such as these, Petitioner can experience worrisome thoughts, distressing feelings, and uncomfortable sensations in the body.

2. This Court finds that owing to these uncomfortable thoughts, feelings, and sensations, Petitioner tends to impulsively react with conduct that can be unproductive and waste time.

3. This Court finds that the growing sense of urgency and procrastination can increase stress, undermine Petitioner's ability to perform optimally, and adversely affect Petitioner's relationship with others.

4. This Court is inclined to deny Petitioner's motion on the basis that additional time will, after a short period of relief, likely result in a similar pattern of conduct, leading once again to distress and procrastination.

5. However, this Court, being a Neural Circuit Court in and for the Great and Healthy State of Mind, has decided to grant Petitioner an Extension of Thyme with which to come to their senses.

ACCORDINGLY, Petitioner's Motion for Extension of Thyme is GRANTED. Petitioner is instructed to, close their eyes, place the extension of thyme underneath their nose, gently notice its aroma, and pay attention to the rise and fall of the breath.

Done and ordered in Chambers this _____ day of _____.

                             _____

                             The Honorable "You"
                             Neural Circuit Court Judge

IN THE NEURAL CIRCUIT COURT IN AND FOR
THE GREAT AND HEALTHY STATE OF MIND

YOU, aka "ME"

               Petitioner,

     vs.

REALITY

               Respondent.

_____/

MOTION FOR RELIEF FROM JUDGMENT

Pursuant to the laws of the great and healthy State of Mind, Petitioner respectfully moves for relief from the unnecessary pain and suffering caused by the never-ending judgments that arise in the mind.

1. Petitioner has been blessed with an intellect and capacity to reason, analyze, judge, and make decisions.

2. Much of Petitioner's prior experience has positively reinforced these skills, especially the ability to make judgments about facts, events, other persons, and Petitioner.

3. Petitioner has survived all prior obstacles and challenges and unconsciously attributes this survival to a panoply of skills, especially the making of judgments. This attribution is in and of itself a judgment.

4. Due to the enormous volume of judgments generated by Petitioner's mind, coupled with there having been positive reinforcement by virtue of Petitioner's survival, it has become impossible to efficiently discern judgments based on law and fact and admitted as credible evidence from those not based on law and fact, or that constitute hearsay.

5. As a result, the incessant flow of judgments has led to circumstances where Petitioner overreacts to circumstances; prejudges; misjudges; criticizes people and events; and interacts with people and treats oneself in a manner that is biased and based on erroneous assumptions — all of which causes undue pain and suffering.

WHEREFORE, Petitioner seeks relief from the unnecessary pain and suffering occasioned by this always-judging nature.

Respectfully submitted,

_____

YOU, Esq.
Counsel for Petitioner

IN THE NEURAL CIRCUIT COURT IN AND FOR
THE GREAT AND HEALTHY STATE OF MIND

YOU, aka "ME"

                   Petitioner,

       vs.

REALITY

                   Respondent.

_____/

ORDER GRANTING RELIEF FROM JUDGMENT

Before this Neural Circuit Court is Petitioner's Motion for Relief from Judgment. For the reasons set forth below, Petitioner's Motion is GRANTED.

1. This Court finds that Petitioner is continually making judgments about everything that arises in Petitioner's mind.

2. This Court also finds that the enormous quantity of thoughts continuously arising in Petitioner's mind, along with Petitioner's prior conditioning, makes it exceptionally challenging to efficiently discern judgments based on facts admitted into evidence from those not in evidence.

3. This Court also finds that as a result, Petitioner will, from time to time and often without awareness, overreact to circumstances; prejudge people and outcomes; and interact with people and treat oneself in a manner that is biased and based on erroneous assumptions—all of which is likely to cause undue pain and suffering.

ACCORDINGLY, Petitioner's Motion for Relief from Judgment is GRANTED. This Order will be SELF-enforcing. Although this Court, being a Neural Circuit Court, is mindful of the challenges (and paradox) inherent in looking to the self to enforce this order, it believes that such collaboration is necessary in order to ensure the long-term relief that is sought.

Done and ordered in Chambers this _____ day of _____.

_____

The Honorable You
Neural Circuit Court Judge

◆

MINDFULNESS CUES

CAN YOU SPARE A DIME?

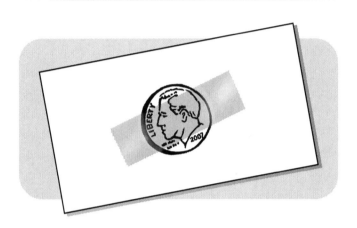

These handy cards with a dime taped on top serve as a helpful reminder to sit and practice mindfulness for a few moments. Used as part of the "Can You Spare a Dime?" demonstration (see page 57), they also offer a reminder of the paradox inherent in a mindfulness practice—that even as little as one minute of practice, or ten breaths, can be so very challenging and, at the same time, constitute a miniscule amount of time in relation to the length of a day.

While you may order a set of these cues, we encourage you to have students select a dime from the pile after your demonstration and make their own cards in class. Doing so, you can creatively add to the exercise by, for example, having them each write down a word on the back of the cue that will inspire practice.

JUDGE-MINTS

These mints, embossed with a clever title and phrase that captures the essence of a mindfulness practice, can be shared with students to remind them of the value of paying attention to judgments.

One of the great mindfulness insights is that judgments are continually arising and passing away, and that without awareness of them we will, among other things, misperceive situations and people, overreact to events, and experience unnecessary levels of fear and worry, all of which adversely affects our decision-making and well-being. These "judge-mints" provide on their face

"Look Inside to Find Refreshing Judge-Mints"

as a reminder that an important shift takes place when we notice that judgments are arising and pay attention. Indeed, by "looking inside" and noticing the thoughts, feelings, and/or body sensations that arise, we experience a measure of relief that, at times, can be regarded as refreshing. We distribute these to students as treats after discussing "judgments" and then share them with students throughout the semester as a way of reinforcing this important insight.

UNCERTAIN-TEE

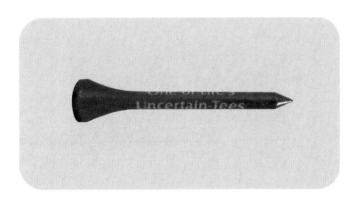

This golf tee work is sized to fit snugly into a small raisin box so that the box appears to be empty. After being used as part of the "Motion to Embrace Uncertainty" demonstration (see page 91), students keep the tee as a mindfulness cue to use throughout their careers. Over the years, many have reported that they keep it on their desk or in their briefcase or purse where it reinforces the insight that they can "bear" life's uncertainties.

EXTENSION OF THYME

This cue, which you can purchase in your local grocery store, is a powerful complement to the "Motion for Extension of Time" exercise discussed earlier in this Appendix. When you begin to distribute the thyme to students, do not let on that it is thyme as students will catch on at varying times and, when they do so on their own, they will be all the more affected by the experiential exercise to follow.

"4–7–8 HANDS" EXERCISE

4 - 7 - 8 HANDS

The *Learned Hand* Exercise to
Reduce Stress and Cultivate Mindful Awareness

Instructions

1. Inhale and Open Hands to the Count of **Four**.
2. Hold Breath and Stretch Fingers to the Count of **Seven**.
3. Exhale and Close Hands to the Count of **Eight**.

Benefits of this Motion Practice

Tone Down Mental Chatter
Relieve an Anxious Mind
Promote Neural Integration and Mental Clarity

JURISIGHT®
Level One
TECHNIQUE

© 2007-2009 Institute for Mindfulness Studies. All Rights Reserved.

This mindfulness cue card for The Learned Hand Exercise known as "4–7–8 Hands" can be handed out to students after teaching them the exercise so that they may draw upon it as a reminder of the instructions or to practice.

"JUST-IS" HOLMES EXERCISE

JUST-IS HOLMES

The *Learned Hand* Exercise to
Cultivate Acceptance and Mindful Awareness

Instructions

1. Gently Touch Tip of Thumb to Tip of Middle Finger
2. Stop. Bring Awareness to Your Breathing
3. Look. Pay Attention to Sights -- Seeing What "Just Is"
4. Listen. Pay Attention to Sounds -- Hearing What "Just Is"

Benefits of this Motion Practice

Stop Overreacting to Unwanted & Unexpected Events
Experience Stillness and Inner-Tranquility
Promote Neural Integration and Mental Clarity

JURISIGHT®
Level Three
TECHNIQUE

© 2007-2009 Institute for Mindfulness Studies. All Rights Reserved.

This mindfulness cue card for The "Just Is" Holmes Exercise, also known as "Stop, Look & Listen" can be handed out to students after teaching them the exercise so that they may draw upon it as a reminder of the instructions or to practice.

ABOUT THE AUTHORS

*S*cott L. Rogers and Jan L. Jacobowitz are co-creators of *Mindful Ethics,* the cutting-edge law program that integrates the classic study of professional responsibility with fundamental mindfulness insights and exercises to facilitate an engaged and transformative learning experience for legal professionals. Together Scott and Jan have taught *Mindful Ethics: Professional Responsibility for Lawyers in the Digital Age* at the University of Miami School of Law continuously each semester since it was first offered in 2010, and it remains a much sought after class. Co-founders of the Mindful Ethics Training Academy, Scott and Jan have presented *Mindful Ethics* in CLE trainings and at national and international conferences as they continue to develop the breadth of its application across different areas of legal practice and society.

*S*cott Rogers, MS, JD, is founder and director of the University of Miami School of Law's Mindfulness in Law Program where he teaches Mindful Ethics and Mindfulness in Law. In 2012, Scott received the Hausler Golden Apple Award, presented by students to a faculty member for their notable contribution to the student body. He has spoken on mindfulness to the legal profession since 1998, and in 2004 founded the Institute for Mindfulness Studies to develop methods of sharing mindfulness practices with different groups.

Scott received his master's degree in social psychology and his law degree from the University of Florida, graduating *summa cum laude.* He served as a judicial law clerk at the federal district, federal appellate and state supreme court levels, and practiced commercial litigation with White & Case during which time he chaired the Education Subcommittee of the Dade County Bar Association's Professionalism Committee. Thereafter, Scott served as general counsel to an Internet company. In 2007 he began devoting himself full time to sharing mindfulness with members of the legal profession.

Scott is creator of Jurisight,® one of the first programs in the country to integrate mindfulness and the law and broke ground offering CLE programs that introduced neuroscience research along with contemplative practices in the legal context. A nationally recognized leader in the field of mindfulness and the law, Scott has taught mindfulness to thousands of legal professionals including lawyers, law students, and judges. He co-chairs the Mindfulness in Law Joint Task Force of the Dade County Bar Association and Federal Bar Association for the Southern District of Florida. Scott collaborates on research exploring the enduring brain and behavior changes that may accompany mindfulness training programs.

Scott is author of *The Six-Minute Solution: A Mindfulness Primer for Lawyers, Mindfulness for Law Students,* and *Mindful Parenting.* He has spoken at law and scientific conferences, appeared on television and National Public Radio, and been interviewed in newspapers and magazines for his work on mindfulness. Scott lives in Miami Beach, Florida, with his wife, Pam, and two children, Millie and Rose.

◈

*J*an L. Jacobowitz is a Lecturer in Law and the Director of the Professional Responsibility and Ethics Program (PREP) at the University of Miami's School of Law. Her program is a 2012 recipient of the prestigious American Bar Association's E. Smythe Gambrell Professionalism Award.

Jan has presented dozens of PREP Ethics CLE Seminars and has been a featured speaker, panelist, and author on topics such as Legal Ethics in Social Media and Advertising, Lawyer's First Amendment Rights, and Cultural Awareness in the Practice of Law.

Jan co-developed and teaches Mindful Ethics: Professional Responsibility for Lawyers in the Digital Age. She has also taught Administrative Law and Government & Ethics. During the summer, Jan directs the Summer Public Interest Program and teaches a Public Interest Law Seminar.

Jan serves on the Public Statements Committee of the Association of Professional Responsibility Lawyers and was recently nominated to its board of directors. She is also Vice Chairman of the Broward Selection/ Oversight Committee for the Inspector General's Office. Jan is a member of the Mindfulness in Law Joint Task Force of the Dade County Bar Association and Federal Bar Association for the Southern District of Florida, the ADL Civil Rights Committee, and a 2006 winner of the Florida Supreme Court's Chief Justice's Commendation for Leadership in Judicial Education.

Prior to devoting herself to legal education, Jan practiced law for over twenty years. She began her career in Washington, D.C. as a Legal Aid attorney. Jan then joined Robert Ades and Associates, one of the first law firms providing prepaid and reduced fee legal services to labor union members. Her career continued at the US Department of Justice prosecuting Nazi war criminals. Jan moved to Miami in 1986 and became a partner in the firm of Dunn and Dresnick, practicing primarily commercial litigation and employment law. She left private practice in 1990 to become a Senior Staff Counsel for American Bankers Insurance Group. Jan began her academic career in 2002 in the Legal Academy of Coral Reef Senior High School and joined Miami Law in 2007.

Jan has a JD from George Washington University and a BS in Speech from Northwestern University. She remains an active member of the Florida Bar and is a certified civil court mediator. Jan and her family have made South Florida their home for the past 26 years.

ABOUT THE ILLUSTRATORS

*C*athy Gibbs Thornton is a graphic designer and illustrator with over 30 years' experience in the creative, advertising, and printing industries. Originally from Barbados, Cathy studied art and advertising in Miami, graduating summa cum laude/Valedictorian with both her AA and BA degrees in Communication Design. She worked as a senior designer, art director, and creative director for large advertising agencies in Barbados and in Miami before opening her own business, CG Graphics.

Over the years, Cathy's award-winning artwork has been featured in several publications, including the *Miami Herald* and the cover of *South Florida* magazine. Cathy takes pride in working closely with her clients from a wide range of industries in the United States, Canada, and throughout the Caribbean region, helping them achieve their creative goals. Her illustrations encompass both traditional and digital media, and her design capabilities include two- and three-dimensional designs. She specializes in logo, brochure, and ad design. Examples of her work in the Miami area include the official logos for the Village of Palmetto Bay and the Town of Cutler Bay, both award-winning competition entries.

Cathy currently lives in Orlando, Florida, with her husband Mike, daughter Natasha, and son Jason.

❖

*N*atasha Thornton, Cathy's daughter, shares the same artistic talents and creative passions. Drawing and painting since she was just a toddler, Natasha has been recognized for her outstanding artistic ability consistently from elementary school through to college. She is the recipient of numerous awards and prizes for her art from local galleries in Miami, statewide contests, and national competitions. Currently attending Ringling College of Art and Design, Natasha received the prestigious Presidential scholarship entering as an Illustration major. She now focuses on Digital Filmmaking, her newly found passion, aspiring towards being a Director of Photography in the film industry.

Mindful Ethics™ CLE Trainings & Recordings

Scott Rogers and Jan Jacobowitz are available to conduct *Mindful Ethics* trainings and workshops for legal professionals, including educators, lawyers, judges, mediators, and law students. *Mindful Ethics* trainings are also available outside the legal context for corporations interested in offering its employees ethics and mindfulness trainings oriented around corporate compliance, limiting malpractice and liability concerns, and general wellness. To learn more about these workshops, contact the Mindful Ethics Training Academy at workshops@mindfulethics.com, visit www.mindfulethics.com, or write to us at:

META

Mindful Ethics Training Academy
Institute for Mindfulness Studies, Inc.
800 West Avenue, Suite C-1
Miami Beach, FL 33139

MINDFULNESS CUES ORDER FORM

Send form to:
Institute for Mindfulness Studies
800 West Avenue, Suite C-1
Miami Beach, FL 33139

COUNT: MINDFULNESS CUE:

_____   "Judge-Mints"

_____   "Uncertain-Tees"

> Purchasers of this book may request a free set of mindfulness cues for educational purposes only. Shipping costs will be applied. This offer is subject to availability. Please allow approx. two weeks for delivery.

_____   "Some of Life's Uncertain-Tees" Card
          (Full Color, 2-Sided Card with Illustration and Motion)

_____   "Landscape of the Mind" Illustration
          (Full Color Card)

_____   "Learned Hand" 4--7--8 Exercise Reminder Card

_____   "Just Is" Holmes Reminder Card

_____   "Just Is" Story Reminder Card

Name _____   Law School _____

Address _____

City _____   State _____   Zip _____

Phone _____   E-mail _____   Class Title _____

For more information, call (786) 239-9318 or e-mail orders@mindfulnesscues.com.

Made in the USA
Lexington, KY
22 September 2017